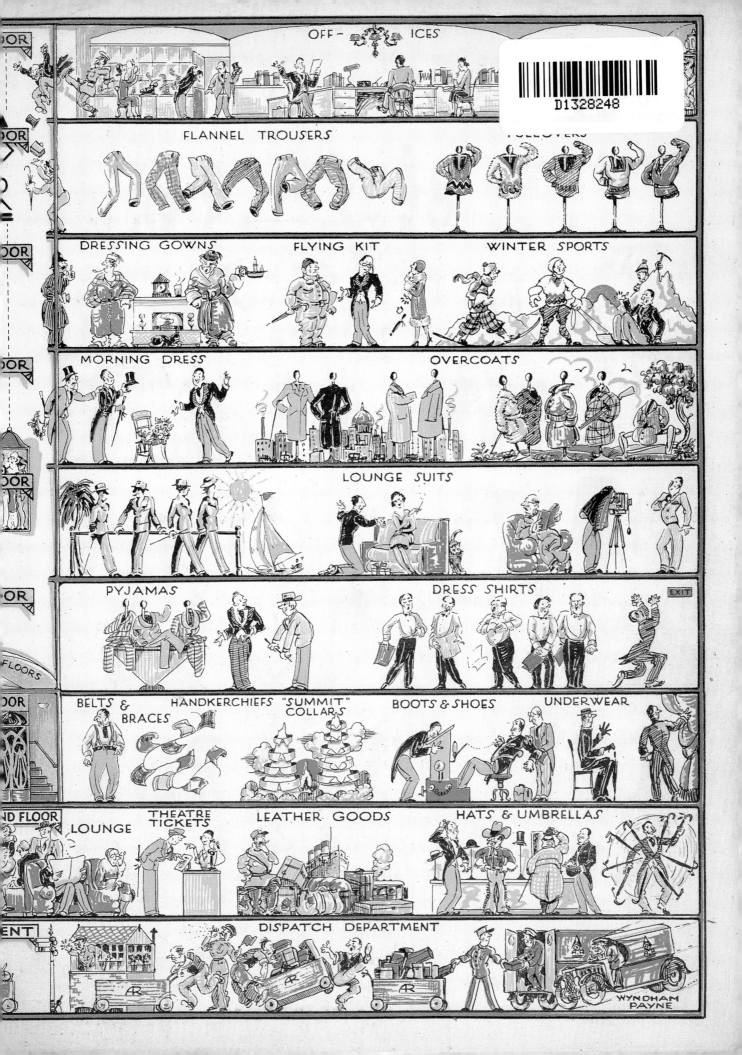

A TOUCH OF CLASS

An Adventure In
REGENT STREET

A
TOUCH
OF CLASS

The Story of Austin Reed

Berry Ritchie

JAMES X JAMES

Acknowledgements

The author would like to record his thanks for their help to David Anderson, Bert Barker, Derek Chidell, Jean Clilverd, Ralph Cook, Doug Davis, Colin Evans, Jack Evans, Jane Evans, Neil Fitton, Gill Hewitt, Philip Horton, Lewis 'Jimmie' James, Sheila Johnson, the late Derrick Kidson, Sidney Leader Cramer, David Pearson, Barry Reed, Laurance Reed, 'Mike' Reed, Joanna Reed-Ödner, Tom Simmonds, John Taylor, Hubert Taylor-Rose, Bill Tindall, Graeme Tonge, Roy Ward, Norman Westwood, Colin Woodhead and last but not least the late Douglas Reed who took a close interest in the early stages of this project.

Roy Dyer deserves special mention for his contribution as Austin Reed's archivist.

First published 1990

ISBN 0-907383-02-5

Designed by Robin Farrow

Originated and printed in Great Britain by
BAS Printers Limited, Over Wallop, Hampshire

Bound by Hunter & Foulis Ltd, Edinburgh

Published by James & James
the registered imprint of Landscape Books Ltd
75 Carleton Road, London N7 0ET

Endpapers and title page: 'An Adventure in Regent Street', one of Austin Reed's early 1930s mail-order catalogues, advertising the nine floors in the newly extended Regent Street.

Foreword

THE story of Austin Reed is threefold.

It is the story of my grandfather, a man who possessed a rare combination of business ability, flair, integrity and compassion, both for his employees and humanity at large. Austin Reed was one of the pioneers of twentieth-century retailing and I am proud to represent the third generation to carry on the traditions he founded.

It is also the story of how a small, family-owned business evolved into a leading UK clothing company with an international reputation for quality and customer care. The Austin Reed Group has been built on principles and practices which I believe are as valid today as they were ninety years ago. This book is a tribute to all the men and women, past and present, who have made the name of Austin Reed synonymous with good value and excellent service the world over.

And, finally, the story of Austin Reed is a mirror of men's fashion in Great Britain throughout this century. The art of dressing well is a subtle one, particularly for men. Austin Reed has always tried to offer its customers a discriminating choice, a touch of class. I hope our story shows we have succeeded.

Barry St G. A. Reed
CBE, MC, DL

103 Regent Street
London W1
March 1990

Contents

Broad Street, Reading, in the 1890s, the location of Reed & Sons' principal shop.

Preface

AUSTIN Reed was a pioneer of modern retailing. He was one of Britain's first 'niche' retailers, building his business on supplying a specific market sector – the clothes-conscious commuter. He was an outstanding salesman, with an absolute commitment to service and value. He was a father of modern advertising, fostering the distinctive use of style and humour which is still a British hallmark. He was one of the earliest exponents of brand names, his own most of all.

Austin Reed was a natural entrepreneur, prepared to take risks and think big. He had that essential ingredient of all great businessmen, a rigorous grasp of the importance of making a profit. But he was also a good employer, earning the trust and loyalty of his employees by his care for their wellbeing and commitment to enlightened employment practice, as well as his enthusiasm.

The company Austin Reed built has made an indelible mark on Britain's high streets. In the last 35 years it has been transformed into a modern corporation under the management of Douglas and Barry Reed, the founder's son and grandson. But the group continues to perpetuate the same high standards of quality and personal service in which Austin Reed himself believed so implicitly.

The story of Austin Reed illustrates, I hope, the contribution the company and its founder have made to British retailing. If it also demonstrates some of the virtues of a 'family' approach to business, from the point of view of employees and customers as well as shareholders, I suspect Austin Reed would not have disapproved.

Berry Ritchie
London, 1990

1

From Reading to the City

T HE traditional start of the Austin Reed story is Saturday, 7 July 1900. This is the date of a handwritten entry in immaculate copperplate which reads: 'Three pounds, fifteen shillings and seven pence.' It was made in black ink with a steel nib in a virgin cash-book, bound in red leather, and totalled the first day's trading under new management of a small menswear shop in the City of London.

The writer was a round-faced, plump young man of 26. Writing the figures gave him an extraordinary thrill. It was his first income as manager of his own shop; not a large sum, but that didn't matter. At last, Austin Reed was in charge! For that reason alone, 7 July is justified as the beginning.

In reality, the opening was the culmination of months of planning. And the words 'Reed & Sons', written in pencil on the flyleaf of the cash-book, contradict any idea that the new shop belonged to Austin Reed himself. It was, in truth, no more than a branch of a well-established family business in Reading. The finance for the new venture had come from Austin's father, William Bilkey Reed, who had put up £600 of his own money as well as guaranteeing the £1,000 bank loan which made up the rest of the working capital.

The idea for the City branch had come from Austin, though, so from his point of view it was his first shop. But even that begs the question of where he got his inspiration.

The story of Austin Reed, in fact, begins a long time before the opening of the small shop at 167 Fenchurch Street. How much earlier is a matter of choice. It could be said to date back to 1853 when Austin's grandfather Thomas, a Cornish emigrant, bought a hat shop in Reading, a market-town to the west of London, after working in Christy's Bermondsey hat factory. But a more apposite beginning might be Austin's early apprenticeship under his father William.

William had joined his father Thomas in 1860, later taking over

Above: A publicity card for Reed & Sons, Reading.

Opposite: Austin Leonard Reed in 1900, when he opened in the City.

9

VOL. XLIV. No. 1,124.

NOTICE OF REMOVAL.

REED & SON

HATTERS & HOSIERS,

HAVE THIS DAY REMOVED their Business from
34, Market Place to their

NEW PREMISES IN BROAD STREET,

Next door to the General Post Office,

Where they trust with the increased accommodation to
merit a continuance of the patronage so liberally be-
stowed on them during the last 28 years.

The remainder of their Surplus Stock will be cleared
at a great reduction at their Minster Street Establishment.

NOTE THE ADDRESS—

100, BROAD STREET,

NEXT TO THE POST OFFICE.

Top: The notice of removal published in *The Reading Observer* on Saturday, 13 August 1881, informing customers of the company's new premises at 100 Broad Street.

Above: A photograph of the Broad Street shop taken at the end of the nineteenth century shows the number to be 99 Broad Street – some years earlier, the General Post Office had commandeered the original number 100 for themselves. Austin (right) and his brother, Stanley, can be seen in the doorway.

William Bilkey Reed and his wife, Emma, in their garden at 12 Howard Street, Reading, where Austin was born.

management of a small hosiery outlet which had been bought in the mid 1860s to absorb his youthful energies. He had also become sole agent in Reading for the 'Registered Perfect Fitting Shirt', an early attempt to develop the off-the-peg market. In 1876 the two concerns had come together as Thomas Reed & Son, hatters and hosiers, and in 1881 William had expanded the family business into substantial, double-fronted premises at 100 Broad Street, next to Reading's main post office in the centre of the town.

William Reed married Emma Bowler, daughter of a local builder, in 1870, and their second son, christened Austin Leonard, was born in September 1873. (Their first, Albert William, died a year earlier at the age of 16 months.) Austin went to Reading School at the age of seven and stayed until he was 15, by which time his father felt he was quite educated enough to embark on life's real occupation – retailing.

Austin Reed had already learned something of the refinements of nineteenth-century retailing. Apart from helping in his father's shop in his time off school, he had gone along for the ride when William took the latest London stock for the approval of more affluent clients at their homes. The carriage trade was still the principal source of custom for most retailers, in the provinces as much as in London.

Now, however, he was to learn what it was really like to work for a living. Early in 1889 Austin was engaged at 5s. a week as cash boy for a firm of hosiers in Ludgate Hill. He was spared the worst excesses of Victorian clerical servitude, recently curtailed by parliamentary reform, but he still had to acclimatize himself to a ten-hour day six days a week, as well as living away from home for the first time. Austin thrived on the experience. Energetic, equable and inquisitive, he

The massive frontage of Wanamaker's in Philadelphia from a series of promotional leaflets about the store called 'Bird's-Eye Views'.

soaked up the business methods of his employers.

Before long he was home again, working in his father's shop. But not for long. Austin's taste of metropolitan life had made him eager for more far-flung experience. Armed with a letter of commendation from the Mayor of Reading, which stated that he was a member of a much-respected family and, more to the point, the worthy son of Worthy Brother No. 1101 of the Greyfriars Lodge of Freemasons, Austin Reed sailed for Philadelphia early in 1893.

America was a revelation to Austin, starting with the salutary discovery that jobs were hard to get. But after some weeks of rather humbling rejection, he found employment as a junior at John Wanamaker's.

In 1893 the Wanamaker store was the world's largest retail outlet. Filling an entire city block with a street frontage of over one-third of a mile, Wanamaker's boasted more than 15 acres of floor space, with 54 departments and up to 5,000 employees, depending on the season. Eleven boilers burned 26 tons of coal a day for the 100 miles of steam-heated pipes, and the building was lit with 4,550 gas-jets and 1,282 electric lights, driven by the largest private power-station in the USA. There were 13 water-powered lifts, more than 11 miles of compressed-air tubes serving 86 sales points from the central cash desk, and seven trucks, 85 wagons and 182 horses delivering as many as 23,000 packages a day. And on top of all this, Wanamaker's had the 'largest and most perfectly organized mail order department in connection with a general store in the United States'.

Austin was properly impressed by the statistics. He was even more impressed by Wanamaker's bulk-purchasing and retail-pricing systems. And astonished by its spectacular shop-window displays.

From Philadelphia Austin went to clothiers and furnishers Hackett, Carhart & Co. on New York's Broadway in 1894 and then, early the next year, to menswear importers Lincoln Bartlett in Chicago. Already he had a good idea of his own value.

Lincoln Bartlett had written rather condescendingly to him at the end of December. 'We will without doubt be ready to use you about the fifteenth of February and if you can arrange your matters in New

Lincoln Bartlett calling cards personalized for Austin.

11

York so that you will be ready to come at that time without disappointing us and be willing to take fifteen dollars a week, which will only be for a short time simply as a trial . . .' Coolly, Austin wrote back on 10 January: '. . . my present prospects lead me to believe that I can materially improve my position in this city in the near future. I will state that I am in communication with Michaelis and Rohman, who seem desirous of giving me an opening. If you could see your way clear to pay my expenses to Chicago, a matter of $25, I should be willing to work for a couple of months at $15. I feel sure that by the expiration of that time I can prove myself.' On 28 January, Lincoln Bartlett cabled: 'Will pay your expenses, please arrive first of month.'

Austin returned home in 1896, rejoining his father and his younger brother Stanley in the Reading shop, where he also discovered a pretty 16-year-old sitting behind the cash desk called Emily Wilson, the younger sister of a local butcher. The attraction was mutual. By local standards, the 22-year-old Austin was a dashing fellow with his traveller's tales and distinctive American wardrobe. He went down well with the shop's customers as well, always so cheerful and attentive to their needs.

His father's feelings were more mixed. Austin certainly worked hard enough, but there was a distinct danger of his becoming too big for his boots. It was gratifying having such an energetic son in the firm, and there was no denying that he had learned a great deal about retailing in the States. Indeed, the benefits were already being felt in the business. Not enough, however, to justify Austin taking over the entire operation – something he was increasingly showing signs of wanting to do.

The situation was not helped by Emily falling ill with rheumatic fever, which removed her ameliorating charm from the shop as well as delaying Austin's plans to marry her. The atmosphere at work became intense enough to upset the rest of the staff, which began to split into two camps, those supporting William and those, the younger, attracted to the more exciting ideas of his elder son.

William was not unsympathetic to Austin's restlessness. He had been through the same phase in his relations with his father. Thomas had resolved the problem by putting his son in charge of a separate establishment in the town. Perhaps the same solution would work again. William suggested making Austin manager of a small branch of the business which had been opened in Reading's arcade. Austin Reed demurred. He had an alternative proposition.

The Fenchurch Street shop had been trading in men's hosiery for over five years. The lease was owned by William Stambrook & Son, East End shirtmakers and hosiers, but turnover was only £3,000 a year and it was losing money. Austin was confident he could do better than that.

William Reed advertised the acquisition of the Fenchurch Street

The young Emily Wilson. Austin and Emily were married on 10 March 1902 at Bridlington, Yorkshire – her birthplace.

lease as a development of his own business in the *Reading Observer* on
11 August 1900:

It is a generally accepted fact that the provincial hosier is a month to six
weeks behind his London contemporary in showing the same goods . . .
A new weave of neckwear silk, an innovation in brace webbings, a novelty
in coloured shirts, a closer folding umbrella than the last closest folding
umbrella is put on the market and the producer of the novelty puts on
his hat and runs round to Mr Cityman who generally knows a good thing
when he sees it. And so the whole first consignment of a new production

The first London shop was opened at 167
Fenchurch Street on 7 July 1900. The window
display shows the early concentration on a
strong marketing story.

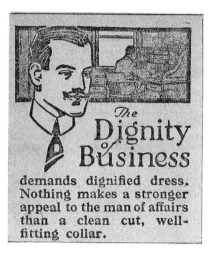

An early advertisement reflects Austin Reed's concern for well-fitting collars.

These photographs are from a special book showing the full range of collar styles available. Customers would flick through the book as it lay open on the counter, and select the shape they wanted.

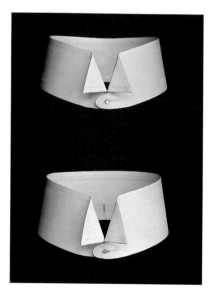

is generally taken up in the City alone, to the entire exclusion of the country trader.

It is in order that we may compete on equal terms with the City hosiers that we have taken a business in Fenchurch Street. We are now at the centre of things, within three minutes of the Mansion House, almost next door to the wholesale houses and in the heart of the shippers', stock-brokers', timber dealers' and tea merchants' district. We are there mainly to benefit our Reading business in order to secure for you, as soon as produced, the newest and best.

The new business will be under the management of Mr Austin Reed.

It hardly needs to be said that Austin had drafted the advertisement himself. It was, after all, merely a résumé of the argument he had used on his father. It was also a rationalization. Underlying Austin's enthusiasm for the City branch was a much more fundamental concept. He undoubtedly felt the Reading shop was out of touch with men's fashion, but his real motive was to move himself to where the action lay – where there was a mass market of young men like himself.

Austin had done his market research. He had started it subconsciously more than ten years earlier as a trainee on Ludgate Hill, but his time in the US had made him overtly aware of the vastness of the white-collar army that flooded and ebbed daily in and out of metropolitan centres. It was certainly true that the new branch of Reed & Sons could supply Reading customers with London fashions more quickly. But it was much more to the point that there were far, far more potential customers in the City itself. And Austin could see, with the sharp eye of youth, that it was these regiments of young men just like him who really wanted the latest thing in ties, the sharpest hats, the snappiest collars, the nattiest cuff-links, the closest of folding umbrellas.

By 1900, Britain was already a nation of city-dwellers, with only a quarter of its 35 million population left on the land. The great bulk of the workforce had been drawn into manufacturing, but white-collar work as a major source of employment was gathering pace. The growth of the colonies – between 1880 and 1914 the British Empire was to gain $4\frac{1}{2}$ million square miles – was fuelling a big expansion of the Civil Service and an even greater demand for clerks to control and process trade, from shipping and shipbuilding through docks and railways to imports of raw materials and foodstuffs and exports of manufactured goods. To service all this development, every major city sprouted its commercial centre, with London the largest of all. And alongside the merchants' new offices were those of the bankers and stockbrokers, raising the capital to finance the world-wide explosion of trade and industry.

Hand in hand with this commercial growth was the development of communications. Queen Victoria had sent messages by telegraph as long ago as the Great Exhibition in 1851 and the telephone was just beginning to make its mark, with the first exchange for private users installed by the National Telephone Company in 1900, while Marconi had brought his patent 'wireless' to the attention of the Post Office four years earlier. The essential medium, however, was face-to-face and any trading house involved in day-to-day business needed to be within walking distance of its markets. And all the transactions, of course, had to be recorded on paper.

The logistics of ferrying the City's workforce back and forth was also being solved. By 1900 railways had transformed public transport, first for inter-city travel and then to the suburbs. The first stage of the Metropolitan Line, four miles between Paddington and Farringdon Street, had been opened in 1863; the District Line had linked Victoria station into the system in 1871; and the Inner Circle had been completed in 1884. The underground had opened up whole new housing areas around London, whose development was also being financed by the City. The Age of the Commuter was firmly established.

The result was a horde of men and women, but mostly men, ebbing and flowing into the City of London, all dressed in a basic uniform

Every day thousands of commuters – Austin's target market – flooded in to work in the City, all dressed alike, barring a few important details. This picture of commuters and traffic on London Bridge was taken in 1892.

15

'The Lieutenant' from 'Types of Men & the Hat shapes that best suit them', an early Austin Reed mail-order booklet on bowler hats. This one 'is eminently appropriate for the vigorous and alert business man of not too big a stature'.

Ties from R. Atkinson, umbrellas from Fox & Co., gloves from Fowne & Dent, collar studs and braces from Welch Margetson – these were the details that distinguished the individual in the City uniform.

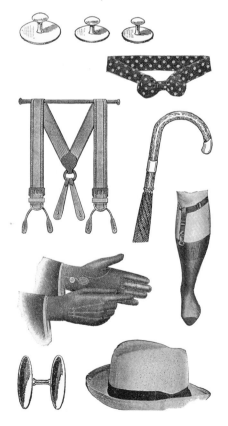

which has dominated menswear throughout the twentieth century. The average man wore a dark, front-buttoning jacket reaching to his thighs with matching or possibly striped trousers, black shoes or boots, a dark hat and, in winter, an overcoat. They were the garments of respectability and affluence. Everyone was expected to conform in dress and behaviour if they wanted to be employed, let alone rise to greater heights of responsibility and wealth.

It was, at first glance, an unpromising, constrained clothing market, the garments differing only in detail. Individuality could only shine through in the cutaway of a collar, the length of a cuff, the colour of a tie, the stripe of a shirt, the discreet gleam of a tie-pin or a cuff-link, the weave of a pocket handkerchief, the length of a scarf, the piping on a glove. But, as Austin Reed knew personally, such subtleties were the very essence of male fashion, positively shouting out pretensions to taste, wealth, power, and ambition, particularly among peer groups of young clerks and their superiors. And he was, as he knew equally well, just the man to cater to the needs of these discriminating customers.

Stocking the Fenchurch Street shop was the first task. It was not difficult. The Reading business had had accounts with most of the better-known suppliers for years, some of which had also exported to Lincoln Bartlett in Chicago, among them underwear manufacturer Allen Solly & Co., glovemakers Fowne & Dent, and Welch Margetson, makers of tie-pins, studs and braces, as well as pyjamas and dressing-gowns. Other initial suppliers of the Fenchurch Street outlet were name-tape manufacturers J. & J. Cash, silk and poplin tie-makers R. Atkinson, shirtmakers Gloster & Co. and Young & Rochester, umbrella manufacturers Fox & Co., makers of gent's socks and underwear Morley & Co. and the Cellular Clothes Company, and hatmakers Christy & Co. and the Panama Hat Company.

The second need was staff. This again was relatively simple; Austin recruited a couple of the younger employees in the Reading store, Albert Wood and Percy Williams. They equipped themselves with a few essentials, like mousetraps, gas mantles, a rubber stamp, needles, ink, blotting-paper, cleaning-fluid, wire and tea – and moved in. Literally. In the early days Austin and his colleagues slept under the counters during the week, only returning to their homes at the weekends. No wonder the new cash-book soon showed expenses for soap, towels and bathing-drawers.

The third challenge was establishing the new business. This was what Austin was really looking forward to. He had some very exciting ideas which he was longing to put into action, now he was free from parental control. But for the moment, just being on his own was enough.

At the end of his first day in Fenchurch Street, Austin locked up

16

the shop and walked the five minutes to the Monument station on the first stage of his journey home to Reading. On Sunday he attended morning service in Reading's Congregational Church with his family, where he gave thanks for what he had received and prayed for God's blessing on his future endeavours. Then he ate a hearty lunch and caught the last train back to London in readiness for Monday morning and the beginning of the second day in the independent business life of Austin Reed.

Cash book of the first month's trading, with entries made in Austin's clear hand.

TOO SHORT!

TOO LONG!

With most ready-to-wear shirts you chance the sleeve length. With Stanaust Shirts your right sleeve length is assured.

JUST RIGHT!

A "Stanaust."

Stanaust Shirts are made in three lengths of sleeve, enabling us to fit your arm as perfectly as your neck.

2

'Making Friends of Customers'

ALTHOUGH the new shop was officially only a branch of Reed & Sons, as the family business had been called since 1896 when Austin's younger brother Stanley had joined the company, there was never any question about who was in charge. It was Austin Reed, and he knew exactly what he was going to do.

To Austin, the retail menswear traders in the City of London in 1900 seemed oddly uninspired compared to those in the United States. Apart from a couple of exceptions, there were few outfitters doing any business of note with a direct appeal to younger men. Austin found it hard to understand. 'Just then we were beginning to experience the first fruits of higher education – a new type of young man was coming into the City – young men of taste and discrimination; men with a new outlook on life, and men to whom new ideas appealed strongly. No one seemed to be giving these young fellows the service they needed.'

From the first he endeavoured to strike a different note. 'We determined to sell the right stuff, but to put a real spirit of service behind every transaction. We put service to the customer – satisfaction to the customer – in the forefront of our policy.'

It was a combination of his father's traditional commitment to good service and the lessons Austin had learned in America. 'You know, it is pretty easy to make a sale, but making sales does not necessarily make customers. Unless your customers go away feeling not only satisfied, but that they have been treated as friends, you cannot create that goodwill between yourself and the purchaser which ensures his return.'

Making friends of customers. That was Austin Reed's secret formula. And not difficult to do, when so many of them were his peer group and shared his passionate interest in the merchandise. But first of all Austin had to attract their attention. Fresh from the New World, where advertising was all the rage, he had plenty of ideas about how to do that.

The first signs of Austin's talent for what would now be called

Above: The company's first logo, *c.* 1903.

Opposite: Austin brought back a variety of innovative ideas from America, one of the best being a choice of sleeve lengths to help ensure a well-fitting shirt. This series of three photographs showing an actor demonstrating sleeve length was used as a window card (which can be seen in the photograph on page 13).

These bowler hats were drawn for a direct mail booklet. The hat at the top is described as: 'The "snappiest" hat of the season for young men – it strikes a happy medium between the conservative and the extreme: while of pronounced shape its lines are obviously correct.'

Getting to grips with collars was a fact of everyday life in the early years of the twentieth century. Jack Weston of Bryce & Weston deserves much of the credit for the early success of Summit collars.

marketing showed themselves in his early window-displays. By the standards of its City competitors, who seemed to view their window space as little more than extra shelving, the displays in Reed & Sons' small Fenchurch Street shop bordered on the dramatic. Items such as shirts and ties were openly presented to view, mounted on stands and clearly marked with their prices.

Austin was also an instinctive disciple of the adage: 'less is more'. His neat mind abhorred clutter and he had a natural talent for striking effects. In the case of his first shop, this economical tendency complemented the fact that, when it came to stock, he had little that could be said to be unique. But there was the 'Stanaust' shirt, which had been made exclusively for Reed & Sons for several years, ever since William Reed had decided that his agency for the 'Registered Perfect Fitting Shirt' was less rewarding than it might be.

As a brand name, 'Stanaust', a contraction of Stanley and Austin, was at least distinctive, if not exactly euphonious. It was, however, the company's own product and shirts were what might be called a core product for which collars, ties, studs, and cuff-links could all be shown as complementary accessories in the window. Indeed, little else apart from hats, gloves, scarves and perhaps socks could with decency be displayed. Queen Victoria was, after all, still alive and such items as vests and underpants, or even pyjamas and dressing-gowns, could scarcely be on public view. In spite of these constraints, Austin's window-displays attracted enough attention to provide a steadily increasing flow of customers.

At the end of the first year's trading, turnover totalled just over £4,000, not a dramatic improvement over the previous management, but enough to cover a £200-loan repayment to William Reed and leave a credit balance of £543. 11s. 6d. One of the reasons for the new branch's profitability was the fact that Austin looked after the pennies to the extent of saying to his hapless colleagues: 'You don't want any money this week, do you?' and keeping their wages as a cash float. They were paid in the end, of course, and they even got Christmas bonuses, but it was a good week when anyone received £2. 10s., including Austin.

The second year saw the fledgling business begin to grow, with sales rising by nearly 75 per cent to just under £6,900.

By this time Austin was getting the feel of his new market. Two years of making friends of customers had also resulted in discovering more precisely what they wanted. Their needs, it emerged, were quite specific in certain areas. For a start, they were extremely discriminating about stiff white collars and cuffs, *de rigueur* for everyone in the City. Not only did the shape have to be just so, but the fit had to be perfect.

Hats were also an important item, especially in early May when the whole City changed over to straw boaters. It was quite a common sight

20

Looking up Lime Street in the summer across a sea of straw boaters.

on a fine Saturday morning to see a long queue lined up outside the shop waiting to snatch a new 3s. 6d. boater, and it was no surprise to sell twelve dozen in three hours.

Shirts, too, were a strong line, with the Stanaust proving popular because it was offered with three lengths of sleeve. Austin's earliest advertising success was a window-card showing an actor doing a Goldilocks-and-the-Three-Bears routine in a Stanaust shirt with sleeves first too short, then too long, and finally just right. This show-card, incidentally, was one of the first to use a photograph, a novel idea for the time. Austin was also beginning to reveal a talent for copywriting, both in his window-cards and in a series of little booklets such as 'Hats and the Man', picturing the range of headgear on offer. The text managed at one and the same time to educate, flatter, and convince – a combination still earnestly sought by every copywriter.

As the business grew, so did the staff. Wood and Williams were briefly joined by a young man called Charles Westwood, who arrived in time to help with the first Christmas rush, then in 1903 by the short, amiable figure of Albert Deane, and in 1905 by a tall, dominant personage called Percy Osborn. His arrival raised the number of staff at the Fenchurch Street shop to unacceptable levels, even by the generous standards of the time. It was, however, a temporary crush. Austin's achievements had convinced his father that the City was the place to do business and within a few weeks of Osborn's arrival Reed & Sons opened its second City branch on the corner of St Mary Axe and Great St Helens, with Deane in charge.

The new branch did nothing to take the pressure off the original shop, however.

Austin talked with his father. William looked thoughtfully at his ambitious son, by then a married man of 32 with a young family of

Albert Deane in 1920. Originally with Reed and Sons in Reading, he joined Austin in the City in 1903 and became the firm's great arbiter of taste and style in his role of chief buyer.

The new and larger shop at 13 Fenchurch Street, on the corner of Philpot Lane, was the first to bear the name of Austin Reed.

his own, and decided that the time had come to hand the family business on to the next generation. Within a year William Reed had retired to Southend-on-Sea, the Reading shops had been sold to a local competitor, and part of the proceeds had been invested in larger shop-premises at 13 Fenchurch Street.

The acquisition of 13 Fenchurch Street was the moment when Austin Reed began to make his name. Quite literally, in fact, as the company traded as Austin Reed from then onwards. It was his name, too, that appeared on the front of the new shop, which was radically refitted to reflect its new tenant's exciting ideas about how to retail menswear.

The new shop was a considerable risk. To staff and stock it trebled salaries and overheads, and refurbishment involved a substantial initial investment. Austin had, of course, very definite ideas about how his new premises should be refitted, based on his experience of US retailing. But to put his plans into effect required professional help. To obtain it, he turned to his ex-employee Charles Westwood, who had recently opened his own shop in Essex. Austin had been impressed by Westwood's fittings and fixtures, which the latter had revealed had been designed by his brother Percy, a trainee architect.

The commission to refit Austin's new shop in Fenchurch Street was Percy Westwood's first significant professional job. It was also the beginning of a lifetime friendship between the two men, who discovered they shared not only a commitment to excellence, but also a sense of humour.

Austin Reed believed utterly in the importance of quality. He always chose the best for his shops, whether they were the clothes he stocked or the environment in which they were displayed. And not only did he demand the best possible workmanship, he expected everything in his shops to last a lifetime – or at least 20 years. Perhaps fortunately, the concept of built-in obsolescence was alien to everyone at the beginning of the twentieth century. The result was that, compared to his competitors, Austin's new shop, with its wide, elegantly dressed windows and its clean, tidy interior with beautifully built counters and fitted shelving, was the epitome of modern style. Customers crowded in to admire – and to buy.

The shops stocked a wide range of accessories.

Austin made sure that his stock was as attractive as his shops. Again his policy was the best possible quality – and at the best price. 'The goods we handle cover a man's every clothing need with the exception of boots and tailored clothes,' he said in 1909 in an interview in the *Advertising World*. 'While building up a large trade in hosiery, haberdashery generally, hats, raincoats and leather goods, we are pre-eminently a shirt house, giving to this department untiring effort and our best thought. We have had the satisfaction of originating new features in shirtmaking and marketing as applied to ready-to-wear garments. Some of these are quarter-size neckbands, different lengths of sleeve, flat-setting cuffs and plainly marked sizes.' (Flat-setting cuffs were expressly designed for the clerk, to avoid his cuff-links falling uncomfortably between wrist and ledger.)

Austin had by then, incidentally, supplemented the Stanaust with the Ambassador shirt and a cheaper range which he called the Summit. After a time the Stanaust disappeared. The reason, Austin explained, was that as the Summit was a name synonymous with peak quality, which he hastened to add it justified, selling a more expensive brand was confusing and unwarranted. In reality, he had unhappily discovered that the Stanaust brand-name was being mistaken for German by an increasingly belligerent population.

He was already using the new brand-name for one of his most successful products, the Summit collar, which he was selling in quarter-inch sizes for $6\frac{1}{2}d.$ each. It was a remarkably competitive price and it was an early opportunity for Austin to articulate his belief in value for money. 'Collars as a saleable article work out this way. The life of a collar is dependent not upon the wear, but upon the continual buttoning and unbuttoning, not upon the rubbing of the coat, but entirely upon the treatment by the laundry. We found that we could combine in the Summit material and workmanship that would stand laundry treatment every bit as well as a shilling collar, and we could produce to sell at $6\frac{1}{2}d.$ singly or $3s.$ per half dozen. So there is no reason to charge more.'

Another popular product range by 1909 was hats. An exclusive series of styles and materials were produced each season, with Austin's Gerrard brand of felt hats increasingly well known, while remarkable suc-

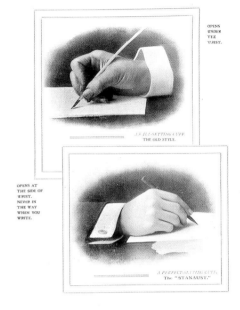

The flat-setting cuff – 'Comfort combined with Economy' – opened at the side of the wrist to make writing easier and more comfortable for clerks.

Below left: Summit collars sold at the very competitive price of $6\frac{1}{2}d.$ each. This early mail-order booklet was sent out to the list of customers Austin was slowly building.

Below: Gerrard felt hats became increasingly popular, with new shapes and styles introduced each season. In this mailing, Austin emphasizes the quality of the product.

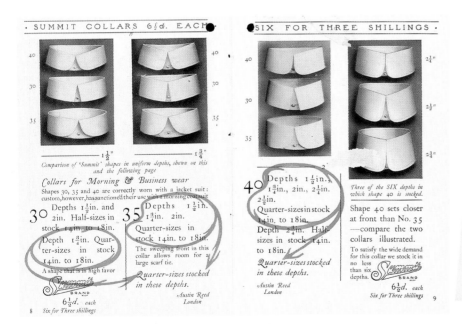

Straw boaters on sale in the new hat department on the lower ground floor at 13 Fenchurch Street.

Austin Reed's long association with Japan goes back to the earliest days of the company, as this window shows.

cess attended straw hats, which in the four months of the 1908 summer season, starting on the first of May, sold over 10,000.

A major reason for Austin Reed's increasing success was sales promotion – again an expression which would have sounded very strange to an Edwardian ear. With constantly crowded pavements outside his shops, Austin took the fullest advantage of the advertising facilities offered by his shop-windows, which he made as bright as he knew how, with fresh dressing in one or another every day and with the most attractive showcards and price-tickets he could devise – all handwritten or printed by his own people. He used what he called 'picture' windows, central displays using a dummy only occasionally, finding them useful for generating general publicity but not so good at producing direct sales. Much more effective were entertaining window-cards.

Austin used advertising from the earliest days of his business. He started promoting the Stanaust shirt in half-a-dozen weekly journals in 1902. By 1905, however, he dropped his media campaign in favour of direct mail, having built up a list of 7,000 past and potential cus-

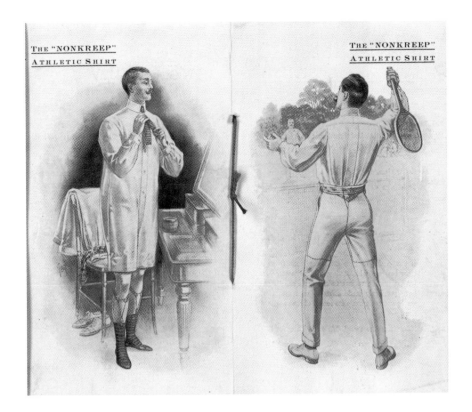

THE "NONKREEP" ATHLETIC SHIRT

THE "NONKREEP" ATHLETIC SHIRT

The 'Nonkreep' shirt 'was modelled principally for the purpose of giving the greatest possible comfort while engaged in recreative pursuits'. The booklet continues: 'We hold that this shirt entirely dispenses with the annoyance usually caused by the tail of an ordinary shirt creeping out of place and presenting that bunched up appearance which creates such irritable feeling whilst in wear.'

tomers from various sources. By 1907 he had abandoned press publicity completely, except for occasional inserts in national newspapers, in favour of cards, changed every month and devoted mainly to shirts, which were displayed in carriages on the Central London Railway and made his company name widely known.

Direct mail, however, was more efficient at generating business. Booklets dealing with some line of goods went out every few weeks, with the whole mailing list covered four to six times a year. The list itself was constantly updated, rising to 15,000 by 1909. Names and addresses were always collected by salesmen at the counters, and every name held on a card was evidence of either a personal visit to one of the shops or a purchase made through the post. The cards were graded by colour to distinguish the class and quality of the goods bought so that Austin could circulate customers most likely to be interested in new lines. Cards relating to inland or foreign mail orders formed another classification. All the cards bore records of purchases, correspondence and printed matter sent.

Austin was remarkably persistent with his direct mail. He was quite prepared to go on writing to prospective customers four, five, or six times, on one occasion finally succeeding in making a sale with his eighth letter. He found the number of mail shots needed varied with every line, with the price being a major factor. But an example was a raincoat retailing at 52s. 6d. Austin used a monthly magazine

These famous goods are
imported by

MACKINTOSH & Co. LTD.

Men's Wear Specialists · HONG KONG

A Day Up the River

is robbed of half its joys if your
Collar gets limp and 'sloppy.'

Summit **49**

is the Ideal Soft Collar for boating wear
—its softness has always sufficient stiff-
ness to maintain a smart appearance.

The eyelet holes in the front
fold allow the Safety Pin to be
fixed without damaging the
Collar, (Safety Pin, 6½d. each.)

Depth 1¾ ins.   **6 for 3/-**

Sample Collar and Booklet 6½d., post
free.

Austin Reed Ltd.

41 NEW STREET, BIRMINGHAM.
" FIVE LONDON SHOPS "

*B'ham 'Daily Mail')
Thursday June 5/13*

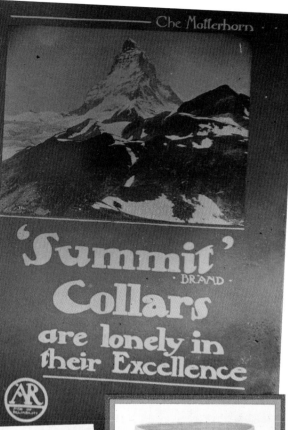

The Matterhorn

'Summit' Collars

are lonely in their Excellence

Summit collars are the ALL BRITISH collars

They are made in one of
the best equipped Factories in
Londonderry, from materials
that are woven in Belfast.

But don't let this unduly influence you. We want
you to get critical, and compare "Summits" with
any other Collar on the Market, whether British or
otherwise. Notice the fine, even texture of the
cloth ; the perfect balance of shape ; the evenness
of stitch in Button-holes and Seams. Measure
them up, and see how true they are to size, and,
best of all, wear them and prove their worth.

All Shapes in
Quarter Sizes. :: **6 for 3/-.**
Sample Collar and Booklet, 6½d. Post Free.

Austin Reed Ltd.

113, REGENT ST. 13, FENCHURCH ST.
5, ST. MARY AXE. 157, CHEAPSIDE.

*'Summit' goods are
sent to you securely
packed—they reach
you READY for
immediate use.*

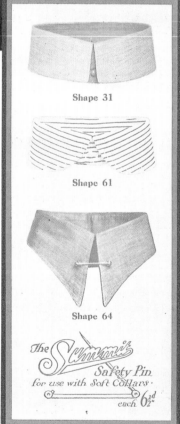

Shape 31

Shape 61

Shape 64

The *Summit*
Safety Pin
for use with Soft Collars
each 6½d

Austin built his reputation on the Summit brand name, used on collars and shirts, and also pyjamas. The poster (*below*) advertising Summit shirts dates from 1910, and is typical of those used on the railways. The dramatic force of the mountain peak breaking through the frame was pretty unusual for the time. Early advertisements were for stiff collars, but Austin soon added the soft collar to the Summit range, ideal for holiday wear. The Summit logo continued to be used for later booklets, such as the 1920s export brochure (*far left*) for Mackintosh & Co in Hong Kong.

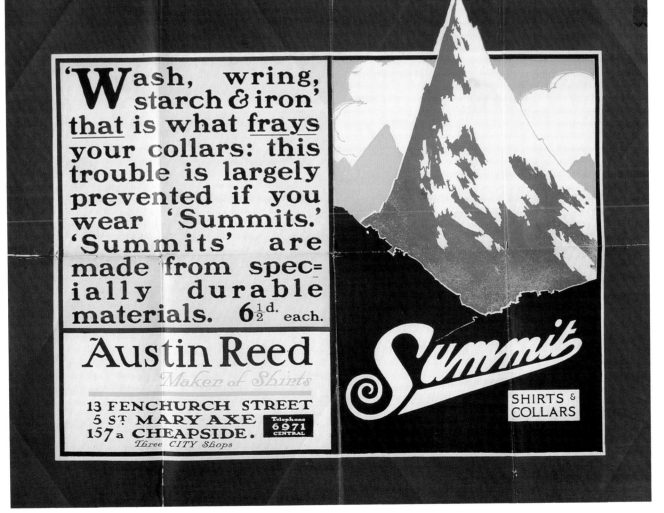

With the advent of the motor car, driving clothes became popular. This advertisement for wind- and rain-proof motoring caps is from a direct mail booklet.

advertisement to drum up enquiries and found that two letters were usually enough to secure an order – the first enclosing printed matter and patterns, and the second seven days later finalizing the sale. Rather more than 50 per cent of enquiries were turned into orders, itself a high level of success, but one on which Austin was confident he would improve when a campaign had run for 12 months. He had no illusions about the need for consistency and perseverance.

The cost of winning new business also made it imperative in his mind to spare 'no legitimate effort' in getting the order, with personal letters vital throughout.

Our growth has been due to the homely features of good goods and a lot of hard work. Efforts all along have been directed not only at making

Another exclusive AR product, the Bracken raincoat retailed at 52s. 6d.

sales but to the building up of goodwill, which we interpret as forming in the customer's mind a friendly feeling towards our house.

Competition looks after the prices; the tradesman himself looks after the qualities if he is building trade in the right way; and there is left service as the deciding factor from the customer's point of view. It is my belief that conditions in large cities are rapidly approaching the stage where good service will play a very large part in securing business.

By 1910 Austin had every reason to believe that his policy of making his customers into friends was right. By then he had opened a third shop in Cheapside and he was already recognized as a rising man in the retail trade.

It was justified. As well as demonstrating his talents as a shopkeeper and self-promoter, Austin had also begun to show his strengths as an employer and manager. This was reflected in the efficiency of his management team. A rather grand word, perhaps, to apply to the motley collection of young men whom Austin had gathered round him in the ten years he had been in the City, but a very real entity. Right from the beginning Austin showed a remarkable ability to make the best of their varied abilities, a skill which characterizes the true business builder. Not all Austin's staff proved able to meet the challenges that his expansion offered them, but he never held that against them. Instead, he gave them a different responsibility, and if necessary another if that, too, proved beyond their competence. Never did Austin blame anyone for his or her limitations, although he was unforgiving of laziness or dishonesty of any kind. A by-product was intense loyalty to the company even among those whose careers were sidelined.

This leaflet advertises hats. The humour of the company's advertising is one of its distinguishing features. Austin is 'making friends of customers'.

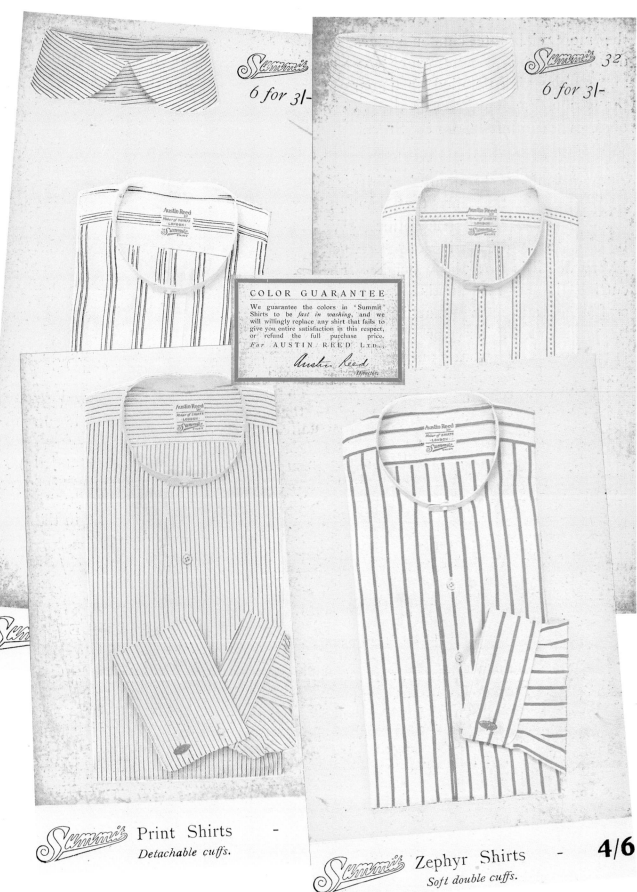

Summit 6 for 3/-

Summit 32.
6 for 3/-

COLOR GUARANTEE

We guarantee the colors in 'Summit' Shirts to be *fast in washing*, and we will willingly replace any shirt that fails to give you entire satisfaction in this respect, or refund the full purchase price.

For AUSTIN REED LTD.,

Austin Reed
Director.

Summit Print Shirts -
Detachable cuffs.

Summit Zephyr Shirts -
Soft double cuffs.

4/6

3

A Very Demanding Man

T HE beginning of 1910 found Austin Reed something of a small business success story. His three branches were all doing remarkably well; so well, indeed, that the year before he had moved his own office from the 8-foot 6-inch square cubbyhole at the back of 13 Fenchurch Street to 19 Nicholl Square, London EC, a modest four-storey building which also provided much-needed warehousing for Austin Reed's increasing stock, which was stored on the upper floors and lifted in and out of the building by a gantry jutting from the eaves.

As well as Austin, the new offices housed Albert Deane as chief buyer, a young assistant buyer called Bone, the elderly and rather eccentric Mr Francis, inventor of a patent ointment, who controlled stocks of Summit collars, Percy Epps, the new advertising manager, 'Willie' Williams, making window-display units, Robert Shorter, who was in charge of window-dressing and display, and the firm's growing secretarial and direct-mail team.

With Deane, Osborn and Shorter, who had joined as a window-dresser in 1907, Austin Reed had, by accident or design, acquired the nucleus of a talented management team. Deane's shrewdness and good taste made him an ideal *alter ego* for Austin. Osborn, a martinet whose terrifying manner was tempered by an underlying fairness, was setting the standards for cleanliness, punctuality and service. And Shorter was already contributing to the presentational flair that so distinguished Austin Reed's shops.

It was perhaps lucky they had all come together as young men. Osborn and Shorter in particular could easily have clashed, the one autocratic and rule-conscious, the other creative and task-orientated. One of the first Austin Reed stories is of Osborn standing menacingly outside the Fenchurch Street shop, watch in hand, monitoring late arrivals of which Shorter, who had worked until midnight the previous evening mounting a lavish window-display to celebrate an anniversary

Above: One of a series of collar advertisements published in *Punch*, all of which are superbly surreal. This collar, one of a new collection for 'the start of the day', provides comfort for the businessman even at breakfast.

Opposite: Pages from an AR mail-order booklet from 1911, advertising coloured Summit shirts. The wide range included over 200 designs, with a variety of collar and cuff styles.

A cartoon of Percy Obsorn from the staff magazine *The Tie*. 'The Staff Major' (as he is called in the caption) was a stickler for neat packing.

of the branch, was by far the latest. Legend has it that Shorter, unabashed, nodded at the watch and remarked amiably, 'Careful, don't drop it,' and that Osborn, in spite of himself, grinned.

The story is probably apocryphal, but it reflects an underlying truth, especially about Osborn, who somehow managed to sustain a ruthless discipline without undermining the loyalty and commitment to the company which was already noticeable among its employees, although most credit for this, of course, must be given to Austin himself. For all his charm, Austin was a very demanding man to work for. He believed in everyone doing their very best and he was not shy about saying so. A constant stream of memos flowed from his office to his managers and salesmen, which left them in no doubt at all about what he expected of them.

It has recently been brought to my notice that all salesmen are not fully conversant with the advertising matter which is issued from time to time. Attached are specimen copies of the full range of advertising matter, and it is specially urged upon salesmen that they will make themselves acquainted with them.

Printed slips have been issued to all salesmen dealing with transactions, discounts, etc. . . . The last line of Section Three clearly states: We cannot accept cheques as payment for goods sent COD. Owing to this instruction having been disregarded we have lost goods to the value of £7/17/10 . . . It is not good policy for a salesman to bluntly refuse to accept a cheque, but he should at all times refer the matter to the manager for his decision. In the absence of the manager, advice should be sent for from Nicholl Square, or from one of the other managers, or in the case of Fenchurch St Mr Marshall is qualified to act.

Advertisement for a new design of collar. Important design details were explained in simple drawings.

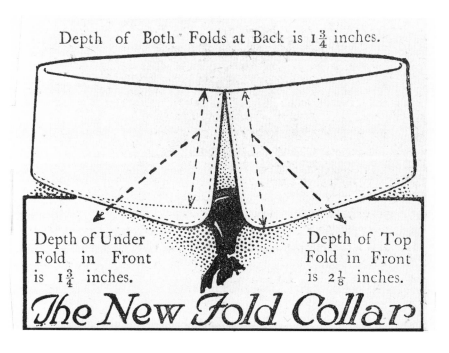

Depth of Both Folds at Back is $1\frac{3}{4}$ inches.

Depth of Under Fold in Front is $1\frac{3}{4}$ inches.

Depth of Top Fold in Front is $2\frac{1}{8}$ inches.

The New Fold Collar

I have this week received a letter from an old and valued customer, complaining that goods bought from us were misrepresented to him by the salesman. I want it to be very clearly understood that we do not wish any salesman to at any time make any statements which will not bear the closest investigation. A variation from the strict truth may sometimes effect a sale, but it cannot possibly be conducive to the upbuilding of the business. A straight question requires a straightforward answer, and it is always better policy to take a swop [*sic*] than to mislead a customer either as to the quality or the nature of the goods he is buying.

Great care should always be taken to get a customer's initials [correct] . . . This week I have received a complaint from a customer who contends that after he has been dealing with us for upwards of ten years, we ought at this time to be familiar with his initials.

Notice: As the collection of carriage on small parcels seems to have led to some misunderstanding, we have decided for the future to pay carriage on all goods. It is, however, very necessary that salesmen should use the utmost discretion in extending this free service. Very few customers object to taking small parcels away with them and, when the purchase is only a small one, the salesmen should not ask the question 'Shall we send these?' When this question is put to a customer, nine cases out of ten he will decide in favor [*sic*] of having the goods sent home and if this is done on small parcels to any considerable extent, it means a very greatly increased item in our carriage account.

House Accounts: Goods had by members of the staff must be in all cases entered on our books at cost price plus 10% and these accounts must for the future be settled weekly.

Soiled collars: For the future all collars soiled by window dressing or by customers trying them on in the shops are to be returned to Nicholl Square and charged back at 4/11 per dozen. Nicholl Square will have them redressed and a corresponding quantity (not necessarily the same shapes and sizes) will be charged back to you, plus the cost of the dressing.

As well as keeping a constant check on the minutiae of management, however, Austin's messages to his staff were also educational.

Salesmanship: The first duty of every salesman when selling shirts should be to take the customer's arm measurement. You may be perfectly well aware of the length of sleeve you intend selling him, but the fact that you come round the counter and measure his arm causes the customer to feel that some unusual interest and attention is being paid him. I find from personal experience very few men realise that they can get from our shops shirts in their correct sleeve length ready for immediate wear. If salesmen will realise that the first step in selling a man a shirt is not to pull out a box of shirts, but is to produce a tape measure and take the sleeve measurement, I feel convinced it will greatly increase our shirt sales.

Humour was often the keynote of internal communication – personally illustrated here by the young Bob Shorter.

Summit Society
Smoking Concert
1910,
Anderton Hotel,
Fleet Street.

Summit Shirts and Collars.
Summit Shirts and Collars,
You can get them when you need
At the Shops of Austin Reed.
So long as you have got a neck
And one or two spare dollars,
You'll look allright
From morn till night,
In Summit Shirts and Collars.

In another man this dogmatic style of management might have aroused resentment. From Austin, so sincerely committed to the pursuit of retailing excellence, it generated only loyalty. No one minded being told how to sell by someone who so obviously believed in its importance – and who did it so well himself.

The same commitment rubbed off on his senior colleagues. Regardless of their personalities, everyone close to Austin reflected his hands-on management style and shared his belief in honesty, quality, and good service.

Up to 1910, admittedly, the management of Austin Reed had been within the scope of its founder and his two closest colleagues, Deane and Osborn. But this was soon to change. The acquisition of the head office in Nicholl Square had involved further investment, some of which had come from outside the family. To formalize the new situation, Austin Reed had been formed into a private company in May 1910 on the advice of Herbert Kidson, head of a Manchester-based firm of accountants, who also handled the issue of £3,000 6 per cent

Yesterday's market-makers queuing outside 13 Fenchurch Street.

The first move west to 113 Regent Street marked the beginning of the company's expansion out of the City. This picture of the original Nash building was taken in 1911, soon after the shop had been fitted out by Percy Westwood.

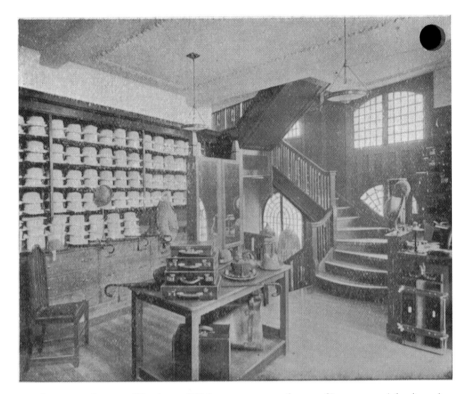

The hat department on the first floor of the
original Regent Street shop.

preference shares. Herbert Kidson was made co-director with Austin,
who was given a 10-year contract as managing director.

The new company was the vehicle for more than the purchase of
the Nicholl Square premises. In February 1911 Austin made his first
move out of the City with the acquisition of 113 Regent Street, on
the corner of Vigo Street and just a few yards away from the southern
end of Savile Row. And a few months later he took over a shop in
Oxford Street. Both were promptly gutted and refitted by Percy
Westwood.

The move into Oxford Street was a rescue operation. It was, in fact,
another branch of Reed & Sons, run by Austin's younger brother
Stanley, who had also been set up by his father, as was only fair, in
a business of his own. Sadly Stanley was not a born entrepreneur and
he was soon in trouble. Austin picked up the pieces, keeping his brother
on as manager.

Below left : Useful dress guidance leaflets were
included with direct mailings and given away
with purchases in shops. This one, from 1914,
went with each tie sold.

Below : Reggie Seldon joined the company
when the original Regent Street shop first
opened. Later he became the well-known
manager of the ground floor in the new store.
He retired in 1959 after 48 years' service.

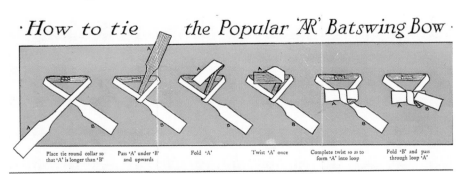

When your laundry comes home

you can see for yourself how 'Color-Fast' 'Summit' Shirts are. No matter how often they have been sent to the wash, from first to last every shade and every tint remains unchangeable—Consider, how much this quality adds to the life of your shirts.

They are made with Stiff or Soft Double Cuffs in Three different Sleeve lengths and scientifically cut neckbands that ensure perfect fit.

Summit SHIRTS 4/6 & 5/6
Two Qualities

Now is just the time to obtain a supply for the New Season. Write for full range of patterns to 24, Nicholl Square, E.C.

Five London Shops **Austin Reed L**td
41 NEW STREET, BIRMINGHAM.

Above: This advertisement for 'Colour-Fast' shirts appeared in the *Birmingham Daily Mail* in June 1913.

A year later Austin bought a Birmingham menswear business called Baugust & Brown, acquiring a long lease of 41 New Street, Birmingham, and reopening the shop in April 1913 as the first Austin Reed branch outside London, also after a comprehensive refit. Six months later a shop was opened in the Strand.

The new branches were not the only signs of growth. By the end of 1913 the mail-order department in Nicholl Square had 60,000 customers and Austin had begun exporting, starting in 1909 with a shipment to Guernsey which was personally accompanied by Percy Osborn. Turnover for the year to 20 February 1914 was £100,000 and net profits had risen to £4,137 after depreciation and expenses. Austin Reed paid a 10 per cent dividend on its 16,658 ordinary shares in issue, as well as 6 per cent on the preference capital, increased to nearly £9,000

Loading the original AR van at Nicholl Square, the company's head office from 1909 to 1925.

The new shop at St Ann's Square, Manchester, opened in 1914, a few weeks before the outbreak of the First World War. It was the second branch to open outside London.

to cover the acquisition of Baugust & Brown, the Strand shop and a 21-year lease on the corner of Exchange Street and St Ann's Square, Manchester. Austin had hoped to open this new shop at the beginning of March 1914, but a dispute in the building trade unfortunately postponed this until the end of May, although when it did begin trading the results were highly satisfactory. That is, until the outbreak of war, which inevitably reduced business in all the branches, as Austin Reed's trade was dependent on just the class of young men who responded most rapidly to the call to arms.

With few exceptions, every employee of military age either volunteered or was called up. An early rush was inspired by Austin himself with a promise, made on 14 August, to pay half-salary to everyone who enlisted by 19 September 1914. Nineteen volunteered, forcing Austin to withdraw his patriotic incentive on 11 September. Two, incidentally, were rejected on medical grounds. 'We are sure they have done all that their sense of duty demanded of them and they can now follow their usual calling with a clear conscience.' A slightly infelicitous turn of phrase, perhaps, but one inspired by his desire to protect the two rejects from white feathers from colleagues ignorant of the reason for their not joining up.

By 1916 more than 40 members of staff were already serving in the armed forces. The company managed to get four managers exempted on a temporary basis, but the only solution to staff shortages proved to be women. After the initial embarrassments these showed that they were every bit as good as men, to the point where they inspired not only keen competition from the remaining male employees, but more than commercial attention from some of the customers.

Many of the new staff were the wives of serving employees, a trend strongly encouraged by Austin. He also made good his promise to support combatant employees financially, paying out £740 in the first

The staff sent Austin a Christmas card in 1915, with photographs of members of staff at home and in the trenches:
'The Summit Boys both far and near
Are thinking of you at this Season of cheer'.
Austin himself is featured on the cover.

Below: An illuminated address presented to Austin by the staff in 1918. This is just one of many cards and presentations which indicate the warmth and friendship that permeated the company.

Presented to *Austin Reed Esq.* by the *Members of the Staff,* as a small token of appreciation and esteem; for the consideration and thoughtfulness extended to them on the termination of the Business Year.
JUNE 1918

18 months of the war to serving members of staff and declaring a special war bonus of £1,575 for the year to 20 February 1918.

Austin Reed's business was affected by shortages of every kind, including fuel for the company's motorized tricycle. The problem of delivery was solved by acquiring a horse-drawn van, which worked perfectly until it was stolen with several hundred pounds' worth of goods inside. The horse, thoughtfully supplied with its nosebag, and van were recovered outside a pub in Soho, but the clothes had gone. There were other hazards. In the first-ever daylight air-raid on Britain a bomb fell only thirty yards from the Nicholl Square offices while the staff was standing on the steps, with Deane pointing out the attacking aeroplanes with his umbrella. The windows were also blown out of the Fenchurch Street branch.

The stock itself became a combination of civil and military goods. In the early days of the war items like shirts, socks, pullovers, ties and handkerchiefs were dyed khaki, sustaining the volume of sales at reasonable levels. But more important to the maintenance of turnover was Austin himself.

> November 4, 1915: We feel that our Brace department could be very largely increased if salesmen would remember to introduce this article and bring it more generally to their customers' notice.
>
> November 5: Re Single Cuff Flannels at 8/6. Will you get your salesmen to push these, instead of the Double Cuff?
>
> November 5: Re Khaki Shirt selling with two Collars at 7/6, this line appears to be going slowly, but the fact remains that it is very good value at today's price. . . We have decided to pay 1d commission on each shirt sold.
>
> November 6: Please note that all Curfew Pyjamas now sell at 6/11 – three for 20/3.

Later on there was a constant struggle to find new supplies of any kind, a task which Albert Deane undertook single-handed, exercising his charm on wholesalers and grateful for anything he was offered. Grateful at the time, at least. Not everything sold. Austin reacted by reducing prices and offering his sales staff commissions for unpopular lines, like khaki cashmere wraps and outsize underwear.

The company also struggled valiantly with wartime regulations. 'We have been pulled up by the Department of Customs and Excise for sending two pairs of gloves to Paris without a licence,' Austin wrote sternly to the Cheapside branch on 24 April 1917. 'Several cases have recently been reported in the newspapers where the transgressing firm has been fined £100 and the manager £50. If we have an unfortunate experience of this kind, we shall certainly expect the responsible manager to pay the £150. Any employee transgressing . . . will make him or herself liable to instant dismissal.'

At one stage the national lack of clothing became so acute that the War Office commandeered the whole of Austin's Nicholl Square stocks. The shortages were inevitably reflected in rising prices. A pair of gloves that before the war were priced at 2s. 6d. cost five times as much by the end; a standard shirt rose from 4s. 6d. to 12s. 6d. and a 1s. 6d. pair of socks increased to 4s. 6d.

The effect of this inflation was to enable the business itself to do surprisingly well. Turnover only fell by £8,000 in 1915, in spite of the many foreigners on the books at the beginning of the war and the large number of customers on active service. The following year profits doubled from £2,493 to £5,088 in spite of the ever-increasing scarcity of material and almost daily variations in prices. Profits rose again in 1917–18 to £7,586, with Austin noting the surprising fact that while increased prices had been partly responsible for the improvement, the number of transactions had also risen. In spite of the absence of so many men from civil life, the business had still managed to attract more customers than ever before.

During the First World War Austin Reed made uniform shirts and collars for the services. These advertisements appeared in *Punch* in 1916.

Austin and Emily having tea during President's Day at the ground of the Summit Athletic Association, in Perivale, in the early 1920s.

Ode to the mail-order department from an early edition of *The Tie*:

'You live on dreams of Owen Nares
    Of far famed movie Queens
Of handsome yankee millionaires
    And call your friends "Old Beans".
Tho' folk may say bad things about you
    What would Mail Orders do without you?'

But running the business became progressively more difficult. Absenteeism became an increasing problem, as employees wilted under wartime diet and the emotional impact of so many deaths in action. Austin reluctantly stopped paying anyone away from work for whatever reason. And it became almost impossible to obtain brown wrapping-paper. In spite of these problems, Austin Reed's sales rose again in 1918. Not so surprisingly they were dramatically better in the first year of peace as demobilized troops returned home, prepared to pay almost anything for good civilian clothes after years of drab and often dirty uniform.

Austin welcomed his returning employees with a memo to Percy Williams at Nicholl Square telling him to issue them all with a book of the firm's rules and instructions:

We have just had a case in which the instructions with reference to cheques have been entirely disregarded by a sales person and as a result the branch may suffer a serious loss. There are a lot of sharks masquerading as Officers, travelling the country and tendering worthless cheques. These men, wearing Military Uniform and a long string of Decorations, easily impress themselves upon the unsuspecting Salesman. No cheques must be accepted unless the customer is personally known to the manager.

Not everyone returned immediately. Bob Shorter, incarcerated in a German prison-camp, did not learn of the Armistice for three weeks and even then only as a rumour because French prisoners and German guards were seen arm-in-arm and the worse for drink. Shorter had been presumed killed in action some time before and his wife had actually sold all his possessions in the irrational hope that this would ensure his return. Other Austin Reed staff were not so lucky. Several were killed and others were wounded. Dick Pierce, for example, who had been the young and cocky fifth man in Fenchurch Street in 1914, lost the use of an arm in the fighting. Austin re-employed him at Nicholl Square as assistant collar stockist to the increasingly erratic Francis.

Austin was forced to raise his prices higher and higher, along with everyone else, in order to obtain stock, but he held to his policy of giving value for money. Gross profits actually fell in the year to 20 February 1919, although the net figure was up. So he was not amused to be accused of profiteering by a customer back from India for increasing the retail price of his three-inch-deep shape 50 Summit collars from $6\frac{1}{2}d$. to 1s. 3d. each. Austin was summoned before a tribunal in the Guildhall to answer the charge, where he was able to prove that his collars were costing him 1s. 1d. to buy, leaving him a mark-up of only 2d.

Austin Reed's restraint on prices did the business no harm at all. Sales escalated dramatically as stock levels began to recover, although the branches were still hard-pressed to meet demand, frequently ending

40

the week with bare shelves. This did not prevent Austin plunging into an immediate expansion programme, with new shops in the City, the West End and provincial centres. To his ever-optimistic eye, the end of the war promised nothing but growth for the economy and the only sensible, the only possible business strategy was to open new branches as fast as could be. Which meant, of course, raising more capital, this time on a scale beyond the reach of his family and friends. With a booming economy and a rampant stock market the answer was obvious. On 31 May 1920 Austin Reed went into liquidation and sub-scription lists were opened for a new public company of the same name with a capital of £350,000.

The first Report and Accounts of the public company formed in 1920.

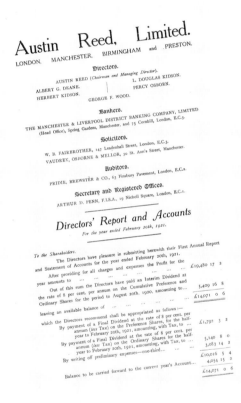

FLOOR			
LOWER	HATS SHOES TOBACCO	SECOND	LOUNGE SUITS
GROUND	HAIRDRESSING CHIROPODY		
	CHANGING ROOMS	THIRD	OVERCOATS EVENING AND
GROUND	COLLARS TIES WRAPS HOSE		FORMAL CLOTHING
	HANDKERCHIEFS GLOVES	FOURTH	SPORTS CLOTHING
FIRST	SHIRTS PYJAMAS		GOWNS MOTORCOATS
	UNDERWEAR	FIFTH	BREECHES PLUS FOURS RAINCOATS
			TROPICAL AND ALPINE WEAR

4

Regent Street and the 'New Tailoring'

Austin Reed's decision to turn his private business into a public company with its shares quoted on the Stock Exchange was mainly due to his need for new capital to finance his expansion plans. Austin had never hesitated to borrow money, but in the past it had always been from friends and business acquaintances like the Battersbys, who had been supplying the Reeds with hats for more than a quarter of a century. By 1920, however, Austin's ambitions had begun to outstrip the resources of this small band of personal backers. He was, as always, in a hurry. He was, after all, 46, no longer as young a man as all that. It was time for action on a large scale.

Going public was an obvious solution. In spite of the war Austin Reed had an excellent profit record, while the company's shops and advertising had made its founder's name extremely well known in the City. Promoting the prospectus was an easy task compared to many new companies, especially with Austin himself as the principal sales-man. Articulate and enthusiastic, Austin thoroughly enjoyed the whole process of persuasion, from boardroom lunches with stockbrokers and their clients to interviews with City journalists. He radiated confidence for the future of Austin Reed with a warmth which was almost irresistible.

Almost but not quite. The post-war boom that had so dramatically boosted the economy was already crumbling and the speculation which had fuelled the bull market shuddered under the impact of higher interest rates. Suddenly all kinds of prices began to fall, from raw materials to finished goods, businesses started to lose money and unemployment began to rise. By 31 May, the closing-date for subscriptions for new shares in Austin Reed, stock-market hopes had given way to an awful feeling that something was very wrong, with the result that the issue was 50 per cent undersubscribed.

The company and its underwriters hid their disappointment bravely.

Above: This logo was launched in 1925 and lasted 30 years. It is a story in itself: at the top is a summit, made up of a white dress waistcoat and the tails of a dress coat; below this is a red lion in a square (for the head office in Red Lion Square); below again the initials 'AR' form the shape of a bow tie, with a dress stud underneath. The two lines at the bottom are for straight trading.

Opposite: The fabulous art deco entrance hall of the Regent Street store which opened in 1926.

Above: The shop in Lord Street, Liverpool, opened in 1924. The original manager was Jack Martin (*top*), who ran the company's business in the city for over 25 years.

A macabrely humorous booklet produced by the company's display department to commemorate the demise of the Preston branch.

In fact they could have done worse, as the overall economic situation slid from bad to worse. By the time Austin Reed came to report on its first year as a public company, the board had to confess that it had missed the profit forecast made in the prospectus by £8,000, a shortfall of 30 per cent.

A year later the trading profits had fallen by another £3,000 to £15,000. Prices for almost everything had dropped unbelievably. A 'land fit for heroes' had suddenly become a country deep in recession. In the circumstances, Austin reported, the company had done well. The established branches, indeed, had actually managed to attract 5 per cent more customers than the year before, while the new branches were doing well. But the volume of sales had only been sustained by severe price-cutting and it had taken 'very close attention to the prevailing markets' and 'the restriction of forward buying to the absolute minimum, combined with every effort to maintain an efficient service to the public' to keep Austin Reed in profit at all.

Austin was nevertheless pushing ahead with his expansion programme as though nothing was the matter. He had bought a freehold site in Leeds, on which Percy Westwood was busy building a new branch, and leasehold premises had been acquired in Liverpool, on the corner of Lord Street and St George's Crescent, both due for completion in the autumn of 1922. Austin was quite sure that shareholders would like to double their 8 per cent preference stock by taking up another £50,000 at 21*s.* per share.

Their compliance was rewarded by a marked recovery in profits the following year, with nearly all the branches doing better than the previous year. The exception was Preston, where business had been extremely poor. Austin was mystified. He poured in all his considerable marketing and display talents, to no avail. Newer branches flourished, but Preston remained stubbornly unprofitable. Eventually Austin commissioned a research campaign, the first ever conducted by the company. The findings were conclusive. Over a given period on a typical business street in Liverpool white collars were worn by 120 male passers-by and coloured collars by 150. In Manchester 170 men wore white collars and 160 coloured. In Preston the figures were three white, four grey, and 24 coloured, with the great majority wearing no collars at all. Bowing to social reality, Austin closed his Preston branch.

Leeds, on the other hand, had started very well, with the branch setting new standards for the company. Westwood's designs for the Leeds branch had been featured in the *Architect* magazine and Austin had proudly sent copies to every shareholder.

Development of the Liverpool shop had been delayed while Austin negotiated a satisfactory property deal. The Lord Street branch finally opened in July 1923, by which time Percy Westwood had turned it into the finest and largest in Austin Reed. In the meantime Austin had opened a new London branch at the Shell Centre on the corner of Kingsway and had snapped up a plum site at Fargate in Sheffield. He had also acquired a 92-year lease in Red Lion Square, Holborn, for a new head office and warehouse. The old offices in Nicholl Square had been under pressure for some years and since the flotation the need for more accommodation had become imperative.

Austin, of course, gave Westwood the task of building the new head office with his usual generous remit. Westwood responded with a handsome modern structure in the style of the moment, which might perhaps be described as monumental functionalism. Summit House, as Westwood's striking, terracotta-clad building was christened, was one of the first examples of a wave of large, confident, stylish developments which included County Hall, the London County Council's gigantic new office block on the South Bank, and the Abbey Road

Above: Percy Westwood, who designed the early AR shops, and (*left*) his drawing of Summit House, Red Lion Square.

Below: By 1920 Austin was already much admired by his fellow outfitters and was elected founding president of the NAO.

Emily Reed officially opened Summit House on 2 April 1925 with (*below*) the key specially designed for the occasion.

Austin on the roof of his new head office, Summit House.

Building Society's towering new head office in Upper Baker Street. Emily Reed turned a silver key in the great wooden doors of Summit House, carved with collars, hats, shirts and ties, on 2 April 1925 and the staff moved in, more impressed than they cared to admit by this evidence of their company's growing wealth and power.

Paper wealth, at least. To finance his developments, Austin promptly took out mortgages on his freeholds. Although property was inevitably becoming an increasingly significant element in the company's balance sheet, he never showed the slightest interest in its value except as a backdrop to his company's real business of selling menswear.

The recovery in the company's profits was not being lost on the City, however, where options on 17,000 unsubscribed shares were quietly taken up at par. By the beginning of 1925 Austin Reed's trading profits were nearly £45,000, Summit House had just been finished after delays due to building strikes and labour troubles, the new shop in Sheffield was open, the Coventry Street shop had been extended on to the first floor, and a long Crown lease had been acquired for the Regent Street branch, where Austin had seized the opportunity created by the lapse of his old tenancy on the corner of Vigo Street to acquire the space for much larger premises. Very much larger premises. A multi-storey department store for men, in fact.

Austin had been gestating the concept of a department store for men for several years. One of the side-effects of floating the company on the Stock Exchange in 1920 had been a more formal management structure, which including putting Percy Osborn in charge of all staff and freed Austin from many of his day-to-day duties. (Austin had also put Osborn and George Wood on the board when the company went public, along with Albert Deane, who had been a director of the private company since 1917. All three of the men who had helped him build up his business, in other words, had been rewarded for their loyalty and hard work with directorships and shareholdings.)

Austin had used his new freedom to visit the United States. He and Percy Westwood had arrived in New York at the beginning of October and had travelled to Boston, Detroit, Chicago, Minneapolis, San Francisco, and Santa Barbara and back via Denver, Kansas City, St Louis, Washington, and Philadelphia. They returned to England deeply impressed with American retailing. There was no doubt that in many respects American menswear shops were a long way ahead of British ones, bigger, better lit, better fitted and altogether brighter and more comprehensive.

In Chicago Austin had revisited Marshall Field, to discover it had opened a six-storey extension on the other side of the street devoted entirely to men's clothing. He also renewed his acquaintance with George Capper, who when he last knew him had run his business from a basement. Twenty-five years later Capper & Capper had two large stores in Chicago and branches in half-a-dozen other western cities.

But it was New York that really took his breath away. Austin had been particularly impressed by Lord & Taylor's fashion store on Fifth Avenue in New York, which on the men's side specialized in ready-to-wear suits, overcoats, jackets, and trousers.

He had been equally struck by Altman's, the 'store without a name', which had been left by its founder to his employees, with its 'quick-service', built-in display units which meant that cardboard boxes could be disposed of, especially for shirts, ties, and gloves. Austin quite approved of the experiment in employee democracy, although he was doubtful about its ultimate success. Then there was Weber & Heilbronner, with 11 stores in New York and very similar to his own business – they had even started at the same time. And he couldn't help admiring the Chain Shirt Shops, where he bought a tie and a couple of Arrow collars and asked the salesman 'How many stores do you have?' 'Sixty-two and more to follow.' 'And how long have you been building the business?' 'Two years!'

And what could he say about John Wanamaker's, which since he had worked there had been entirely rebuilt with wonderful interiors, gave organ recitals throughout the day on the world's largest pipe-organ, and closed at 5.10 p.m. with a fanfare played by trumpeters standing on the balcony outside! Back home Austin's own shops appeared small, dingy, dull and badly lit in comparison.

Westwood was equally inspired by the trip and Austin Reed's branches, both old and new, immediately began to reflect the lessons learned. The shops and windows became more brightly lit and Westwood's own variation on 'quick-service' fixtures were designed, installed, tested in service, adapted and finally standardized throughout the branches.

Progressively, too, the new branches grew in size as Austin revised his old philosophy of 'small is beautiful' and sought out ever-larger premises. Bigger shops meant bigger stock. Austin had the answer to this, although it took him until the beginning of 1925 to satisfy himself that he had the formula right to launch the 'New Tailoring'.

The New Tailoring was Austin's euphemism for ready-to-wear clothing. Unlike America, where almost everyone wore ready-to-wear suits, in the UK only the poorer professional classes wore off-the-peg clothing. Anyone with social pretensions had his suits hand made. The rich went to Savile Row, where they were served by an élite dedicated to perfection of cut and fit. The less well-off patronized popular made-to-measure tailors such as Montague Burton, the Fifty Shilling Tailors and Hepworths. There was mass-produced ready-to-wear clothing, but it was crudely cut from cheap, heavy fabric in an all-too-obviously limited range of shapes and sizes.

What marked the New Tailoring out from the rest of the ready-to-

The New York skyline sketched by Percy Westwood on his visit to the United States with Austin in 1920.

One of the ideas Austin brought back from the US was the use of neon lighting. This neon display lit up the Sheffield store in 1924.

THE NEW TAILORING

BUSINESS SUITS
In Grey Pin-head Worsted

5 & 6 guineas

One of a series of Tom Purvis posters used to promote the New Tailoring in 1926. Purvis designed posters for a variety of companies, including Dewar's Whisky, Bovril, LNER, Shell-Mex and BP.

A view from Piccadilly, looking up the Regent Street that Nash built. This picture was taken in 1912, a year after Austin Reed moved into number 113, to the left of the dome.

wear market was its quality and the wide range of fittings. Before he introduced it, Austin had long talks with potential suppliers, especially John Barran. Between them they evolved a system which gave customers the attractive combination of a choice of the very best cloth, good workmanship, the latest styles, and over a hundred fittings. On top of that Austin added an alteration service which meant that it was a rare figure of a man who could not find an example of the New Tailoring that fitted him.

In fact, most customers discovered that Austin Reed's off-the-peg suits often looked better than the ones they had been buying from their bespoke tailors, while the quality and the finish were just as good – and the price considerably less.

The New Tailoring was put under the direction of Captain C. H. Hills MC, an ex-regular army officer who had joined Austin Reed in 1922, and introduced gradually throughout the group's branches. It took time and money. Selling-space had to be created for the new departments, which also had to be provided with changing-rooms. Staff had to be trained to demonstrate the range of cloth available and advise on weight and suitability for various uses and climates. They also had to learn to measure customers discreetly but accurately and master the far from trivial business of alterations.

The New Tailoring took time to catch on. British middle-class prejudice against ready-made suits proved hard to dislodge. However, persistent advertising and sales promotion gradually overcame market resistance.

Much more instantaneous success attended Austin's other major US-derived innovation, which was no less than the creation of the first UK menswear department store. It was the redevelopment of Regent Street that gave Austin his opportunity.

Regent Street was originally designed by John Nash as part of plans drawn up by the great architect in 1811 for the development of Regent's

Park. The buildings he created along the 'New Road' from the park into the centre of London's West End, and particularly the curving arcaded terraces on what was initially called the Quadrant, the section immediately above Piccadilly Circus, became justly famous as some of the most inspired architecture of the nineteenth century. By the end of the 1900s, however, it was obvious that Regent Street needed to be redeveloped. As early as 1894 the Royal Institute of British Architects was being told that

> The little shops, once so ample, had had to take in not only the back parlours, but every inch of back gardens; what had been kitchen offices were now warehouse basements; and as for the residential accommodation above, not only had it been abandoned in that capacity, but a new tenant would give as much for the shop alone as for the entire house, so that the upper stories, with their miserable staircases, were either utilised for workrooms and storage, or let off contemptuously ... All this time the structural stability of the houses, never good, had been so tried by alterations that public attention was now and then called to the appearance of danger; and as for sanitary questions, the least said the better.

Right from the beginning, however, the 'centennial redevelopment' was a matter of violent debate, with open conflict between the Crown's desire for a uniform building scheme and retailers' insistence on practical accommodation. The answer, it was hoped, lay in commissioning another eminent architect capable of emulating Nash. The choice was Norman Shaw, famous for houses in Chelsea and the country and for New Scotland Yard. Shaw's designs for the area including the terraces were displayed at the Royal Academy in 1906, where they attracted vehement criticism from Regent Street's shopkeepers, who disliked the height of the buildings, the colonnades separating the windows and the fact that they were to be built in costly Portland stone. Several years later the row was still dragging on. Finally in 1916 Sir Reginald Blomfield was effectively given the job of redesigning Shaw's grandiose scheme and became the man most responsible for the 'new' Regent Street, although by no means the only architect involved.

The delay had at least had the advantage of allowing the controversy to lose its virulence, while the post-war boom had widened retailing ambitions. Blomfield made considerable changes to Shaw's original proposals, but much of their character remained. The windows were more practical and the overshadowing pillars were disciplined or banished. But the Portland stone was kept, as was the grandeur and the unified sweep along both sides of the Quadrant.

Austin Reed's existing Regent Street branch, on the corner of Vigo Street, was on the northern tip of the concave western terrace. Like all the other tenants, Austin was given the choice of getting out or putting up with the redevelopment in return for a new lease. He had

The Regent Street shop continued trading throughout the rebuilding programme, with other properties being demolished around it. Austin Reed never lost a day's trading!

Looking up the central well to the ceiling of the third floor from the ground. The metalwork balconies incorporated the Summit motif, and the whole well was shaped like a wing collar.

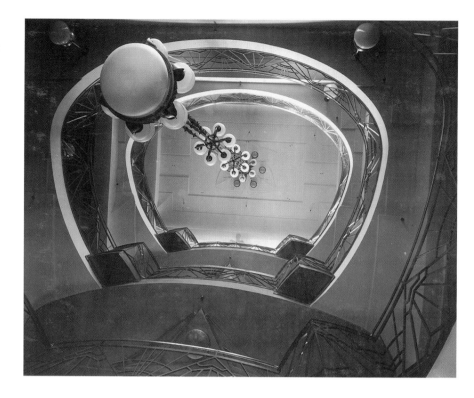

'To dress badly when one might dress well may be arrogance – or mere laziness – a laziness by which one is unfavourably judged. Who is so sure of himself that he dare take the risk? And why take any risk unnecessarily? The New Tailoring at Austin Reed's makes it so easy to be well dressed.'

no doubt about what to do; the only question was how much he could afford to extend his premises in what was undoubtedly going to be the grandest metropolitan shopping mall in the UK.

Not that he was unaware of the risk he was taking. It meant raising the preference capital by another £150,000 – a very big investment but one which he was sure would quickly be justified. His hopes, however, that he would be able to move into the new premises in little more than a year from signing his new lease were dashed by rebuilding delays which held back the opening until the autumn of 1926.

In fact the redevelopment was carried through at a remarkable pace. Austin Reed's Regent Street business was also maintained, as the new building was erected round the old branch which Austin occupied until the very last moment, moving overnight into the completed section of his new, larger premises so that trading never actually ceased.

The new buildings were very much more substantial than the old Nash terraces. Deep foundations resulted in spacious basements, while steel-framing meant wide spans and lofty ceilings on all the upper floors.

The structures and exteriors may have been Blomfield's but the interiors were the responsibility of the tenants. It was the opportunity for Percy Westwood to demonstrate what shop-fitting should really amount to. He let his imagination run riot. He was up against some impressive competition; Austin Reed wasn't the only retailer with a commitment to quality and a leaning towards the lavish; all the way up Regent Street interiors were being fitted out regardless of expense, culminating in Captain Stewart-Liberty's half-timbered fantasy, built with wood from the old HMS *Hindustan* and HMS *Impregnable*, at the other end of the street.

There was no way Austin Reed was going to be left behind. Right from the start the emphasis was on excellence and distinction, combined with Austin's continuing conviction that everything should last for at least 20 years. Percy journeyed to distant quarries to choose marble and stone and to the East End timber-yards to select the wood for the new store, where he handpicked every veneer and chalk-marked individual pieces for especially important items, such as doors or drawer-fronts. Equal care was taken in choosing all materials, from marble floorings and bronze fitments to carpets, curtains, and other furnishings.

The new, distinctive Regent Street store, awaiting the finishing touches.

To ensure the best results, extraordinary care was taken over details. Even the nails fastening the floor-boards in the Tudor rooms were hand-made to look genuine.

Mock Tudor was a weakness of the 1920s, reflecting the continuing influence of late-Victorian architects like Norman Shaw. Rows of 'Tudor' semis were concurrently being erected along the arterial roads radiating out from the cities into the new suburbs. But in Austin Reed's new store, at least, the reproductions were in the best possible taste. The Tudor rooms on the fourth floor, for the record, were the setting for sports clothes and men's dressing-gowns. Perhaps the association was with draughty Elizabethan country houses.

The 'ghost' of Byron on the stairs of the Tudor galleries, part of the opening promotion.

The ground floor was given over to collars, ties, gloves, handkerchiefs and other accessories, while the first floor contained shirts, pyjamas, and underwear. The New Tailoring was housed on the second floor, and dress clothing on the third in the Ballroom Corner. The fourth and fifth floors contained the Tudor galleries, selling country clothes, rainwear, motoring clothes and sportswear. The centre-piece of the new Austin Reed store, however, was the great oval entrance hall, reaching up to the ceiling of the third floor, with its art deco balconies (in the shape of wing collars) and lift-shaft by the sculptor Joseph Emberton.

The tone throughout was 'gentlemanly', a word which precisely reflected Austin Reed's customer profile. It was a subtle and peculiarly English definition which Austin understood perfectly and on which he had built his business. He recognized the state in himself; like every other aspiring middle-class Englishman, he knew that one really had to be born a gentleman and to be in any form of trade or commerce was a disqualification, but at least one could dress like one. He was far too shrewd not to recognize that the concept was a delusion. What his customers really wanted was to dress in a manner befitting the successful professionals which so many of them were becoming. But the

Austin (right) with Lord Dewar walking down Regent Street after the opening of the new store.

self-image of Britain's aspiring middle classes was confused by the fact that their country still ruled over the largest empire the world had ever seen. Indeed, a significant percentage of Austin Reed's customers were doing the ruling. And appearing a gentleman was implicit in the colonial job-description.

Austin Reed had been building a substantial mail-order business with expatriate customers for years, but the new Regent Street store gave the company room to specialize in tropical outfitting. Austin also capitalized on the need of many colonials for fashionable wardrobes in which to enjoy the pleasures of home leave – Ascot, Lord's, Henley, Wimbledon and so forth. A whole section of the company's marketing was aimed at this upper-crust leisure-market.

The day finally dawned for the official opening of the new store. Flushed with pride, Austin planned a grand occasion, which was nearly marred by last-minute delays. But Austin made a personal appeal to the mixed workforce of builders, electricians, carpenters and shop-fitters, and a tremendous all-night effort saw the new store completed just in time.

Guests were invited to foregather on the fifth floor at noon for a tour of the new premises. By one o'clock they had congregated in the entrance hall on the ground floor. Suddenly there was a fanfare of trumpets from a balcony, *à la* Wanamaker's, the signal for Austin Reed to step forward and introduce the guest of honour, Lord Dewar, who he explained had graciously agreed to open the new store to the public.

The official opening of the rebuilt Regent Street on 23 June 1927; King George V and Queen Mary drive past cheering crowds. The new Austin Reed building is at the end of the left-hand sweep. It is just possible to make out the Summit decorations at first floor level.

Guests at the opening flooding out of the store en route to lunch at the Café Royal. On either side, members of the public are eager to enter the new store.

Smiling, the noble lord unlocked the great bronze door and flung it open with a flourish. Or rather tried to. Unfortunately the top bolt was still closed and Lord Dewar nearly dislocated his shoulder, to the mingled concern and mirth of his audience. It took but a moment, however, to remove this last barrier to Austin Reed's greatest achievement to date.

PROCEDURE AT
The Opening
OF THE
New Austin Reed Building
105-113 REGENT STREET W.1
BY
The Right Hon.
THE LORD DEWAR, J.P., D.L.

Austin Reed at the centre of the top table, with Lord Dewar on his right, during the Café Royal lunch to celebrate the opening of the new store, on 25 October 1926. Emily is at the top of the centre table on the right.

MODERN
MAN

AUTUMN   1929   PRICE 6d

5

Modern Man

T HE guests at the celebratory luncheon at the Café Royal on 25 October 1926 were a measure of how far Austin Reed had come. For a start there were his retailing peers, among them Sir Thomas Lipton, the yachting grocer, and Gordon Selfridge, the founder of the famous department store on London's Oxford Street. Then there was a sprinkling of peers, two privy councillors, three MPs, and a dozen knights, plus the Mayor of Westminster and the Dean of Windsor. Sir Reginald Blomfield was also justifiably present, supported by Percy Westwood.

Some of the guests on the top table were doing more than just eating Austin's lunch. They were publicly applauding his new store as well. These special supporters included the Rt. Hon. T. P. O'Connor, PC, MP, Sir Robert Donald, GBE, Robert Hale, and the romantic novelist Jeffery Farnol. All four had lent their names, and their writing skills, to a series of advertisements, each headed 'An Impression of the New Austin Reed's in Regent Street', which Austin was running in the national press. O'Connor wrote a straightforward eulogy of the new store. Donald conjured up Thomas Carlyle in his panegyric on the Philosophy of Clothes, the Spirit of Tailoring, and the Cult of the Dress-Coat. Hale's contribution tried to be funny. And Jeffery Farnol's lengthy effusion fully reflected the author's ability, so admirably demonstrated in such romantic fictions as *Sir Isumbras at the Ford*, to allow the genius of imagination to pervade the commonplace.

Presumably all were customers of Austin Reed, although whether they were paid in cash or in kind for their efforts is not recorded. Their support had been enlisted by Austin Reed's advertising manager, Donald McCullough, as part of a co-ordinated marketing campaign that he had devised with the aid of Pritchard Wood, the advertising agency.

The 'advertorials' reflected a return to press promotion by Austin

Above: Fougasse's whispering men became a well-known AR symbol.

Opposite: The cover of the first edition of *Modern Man,* a seasonal magazine mailed to AR's ever-increasing clientele at home and abroad.

Advertising cards were widely used in the carriages of London's underground.

Reed, which for so long had relied almost entirely on direct mail, cards on public transport and in-store promotions. Austin was persuaded that his company had grown large enough to benefit from a more sophisticated approach. From the 1920s onwards advertisements for Austin Reed appeared regularly in magazines such as *Punch*.

But he was still chary of indiscriminate advertising. Instead, he encouraged McCullough to improve the company's own promotional material. McCullough responded by commissioning the best artists and copywriters he could find to promote the firm's image. One of the most outstanding was the artist Tom Purvis, who incidentally was also a guest at the Café Royal lunch, although seated at the end of a side-table. Purvis specialized in strong, simple illustrations of tall, well-dressed men which did more to formulate an impression of style at Austin Reed than anything else. Other leading illustrators, like E. McKnight Kauffer and Theyre Lee-Elliott, the designer of the BOAC 'Speedbird', also produced posters and other promotional material for Austin Reed.

From the autumn of 1929 this included *Modern Man*, a 'masculine magazine', which was published with a cover price of 6*d*. The first issue contained articles on the difficulties of being a model, outboard motor-boats, cheating at cards and Harris tweed, a jokey column or two about dress and manners, and advice on flying-clothes and tropical kit, the last by 'a district commissioner'. The text had a consistency which revealed that it was largely the work of the editor (McCullough). The style reflected the self-consciousness of the British male about the whole subject of how to dress properly. On the one hand it showed the deep-seated fear, common to every middle-class Englishman then and now, of not wearing the right thing; on the other an equally fundamental reluctance to admit to having any doubts, let alone worrying about them. The result was a facetiousness typical of the period, which was parodied so mercilessly by P. G. Wodehouse.

In fact *Modern Man* soon evolved into little more than a brochure, its editorial increasingly promotional. Its success in this role was

AR raincoats were tough enough to do battle with the elements.

reflected in the survival of the title into the early 1950s. But its contribution to public awareness of the Austin Reed name was limited.

Luckily it did not matter. A much more powerful talent was at work on Austin Reed's behalf. As a young man Kenneth Bird was an outstanding all-round athlete, a champion boxer and the scorer of the only try in the Scottish Rugby International trials in 1913. But he was invalided out of the Army in 1915 with a shattered back and spent five years before being able to walk again. During the time he was in hospital his wife, herself an artist, encouraged him to learn to draw, and eventually his first cartoons began to appear in *Punch*, signed Fougasse. Bird's genius, both as a humorist and a cartoonist, rapidly established his reputation. He continued to draw for *Punch*, making a major contribution to its success and eventually becoming the editor. During the Second World War his series of posters for the Ministry of Information, 'careless talk costs lives', made the Fougasse name world-famous.

Few businessmen, however, could persuade Bird to lend his skills to promoting their products. Austin was one of the exceptions, largely because they shared a similar generous sense of humour. Fougasse's talent was remarkable in many ways, but perhaps particularly for the kindliness of his cartoons, especially marked in comparison with today. Fougasse's work made friends for Austin Reed all over the world.

Fougasse's wonderful sense of humour and distinctive style permeated the company's advertising during the 1930s. The popular card *below* appeared on the underground system. The majority of cartoons appearing in this and the subsequent chapter are by Fougasse – all drawn for AR sales literature.

The new store in Regent Street proved every bit as big a draw as Austin had hoped and within two years of its opening profits had risen to a record £80,000 – thanks in part to the fact that for virtually the first time in its history, and certainly since it went public, the company had all its capital employed. Austin didn't let that last. By the beginning of 1929 he was already negotiating for the leases of the shops next to his in Regent Street, extending his superstore further towards

Sir Alan Cobham (left), and Austin presenting Lady Cobham with a red lacquer coffee set at the opening of the Red Lacquer Room. Wearing a topee is 'Jimmie' James, later to become a post-war general manager of the store.

Piccadilly Circus. Percy Westwood and his sons Bryan and Norman were soon hard at work refurbishing the extensions in even more imaginative style; a Louis XV room for bespoke shirts and, the *pièce de résistance*, a tropical room with murals of the Empire and carved red lacquer screens from Peking. Austin recruited the aviation pioneer Sir Alan Cobham to officiate at the opening, which was another good excuse for publicity and a party.

The fact that Austin Reed had lavished so much effort on a special department catering exclusively for Britain's colonial administrators and their families reveals, incidentally, how valuable this niche-market had become. The truth was that it constituted the marketing man's dream – a clearly defined target audience with specialist needs and a high disposable income unaffected by the swings and roundabouts of the British economy.

The expatriates serving in India were an especially exploitable market segment. There were only about 300,000 of them to rule a nation of 350 million, but they earned monthly salaries ranging from £60 to a fantastic £400, not to mention clothing allowances for the varied and bizarre wardrobes their status-conscious employment required. Just how strange this could be was revealed by the 'district commissioner' in *Modern Man*:

Even in the matter of head-dress, fit and weight are worthy of considera-tion. Given a tropical sun and a heavy ill-fitting pith helmet, and you have an oven that would cook an egg. It is capable of giving the wearer a heatstroke or making him as bald as a billiard-ball.

In tropical sunshine, thin, light-coloured clothing is generally regarded as being hotter than that made of thicker and darker material. It is for this reason that bush shirts, worn with a spine pad, are made of brown flannel. It is supposed to protect the body from the rays of the sun and there is probably something in this theory.

When horse-riding in the tropics I usually wear sokotos – khaki knickers rather like rowing-pants, except in colour – and socks. When going through thick bush, on the other hand, I prefer knee-breeches and puttees. The riding 'get-up' leaves a bare leg from thigh to the top of the sock, and for the first few days there is no doubt about the blisters, but after a time the costume is delightfully free and comfortable.

The credentials of the anonymous author as an expert on both climatic and social hazards in the hotter parts of the Empire were established by his opening remarks.

In my little life I have seen many Britishers make their bow to the tropics, but few however were properly dressed for the part. One man – I know his grave well – landed with a straw hat and case of whisky. 'I believe in travelling light,' he said, 'and I believe in keeping well-oiled.' Another – now a tame master at a very new prep school in the South of England – startled us with a colour scheme that was more lurid than a native anecdote. It would have been all right for the Chelsea Arts Ball, but was beyond the self-control of our simple-minded mess.

The suspicion that the real author had never been further east than Paris strengthens with the article's culminating advice that 'undoubtedly the wisest course for anyone about to leave for the tropics – or

Painted by Fred Taylor, these Empire murals were especially commissioned by the company for the Red Lacquer Room. *Above left* is a magnificent state procession in India; *above* a reconstruction of HRH the Prince of Wales receiving the chieftains of West Africa in 1925.

Expatriates being welcomed in the Tropical Department.

Going OUT?

or Going BACK?

An advertisement for the Tropical Department which appeared in *Punch*.

out East if you prefer it – is to put himself in the hands of the expert provided by a really reliable firm of men's outfitters who run a tropical department.'

Fortunately, the men who staffed Austin Reed's tropical department could be relied on to know what was suitable; from a range of hard-wearing and practical garments for the extremes of climate which could be expected, especially in India, where the dry heat of the desert States contrasted with the humidity of the southern monsoon or the bitter cold of the North-West Frontier. Perhaps even more vital was Austin Reed's confident expertise about social matters; morning clothes for Government House garden-parties; black dinner-jackets for the winter and white for the summer; what gloves to wear and when; what hats; what shoes; what ties . . .

Austin Reed made quite sure that everyone who travelled to and from the colonies knew about its capabilities. In due course each of India's 300,000 were circulated, while an Austin Reed advertisement appeared fortnightly in *The Statesman*, India's leading English-language newspaper. And every passenger on every P & O liner from the East received an invitation to visit Regent Street. If they took it up – and many did – they were greeted personally by Mr Bright, the manager of the India department in the Red Lacquer Room, who bent over backwards to replenish their tropical kit. He was a positive guru on the subject of clothes, conditions, and customer credit arrangements, including subscription accounts.

The shaded countries are those from which Fred Taylor drew the inspiration for his friezes (on pages 58–9).

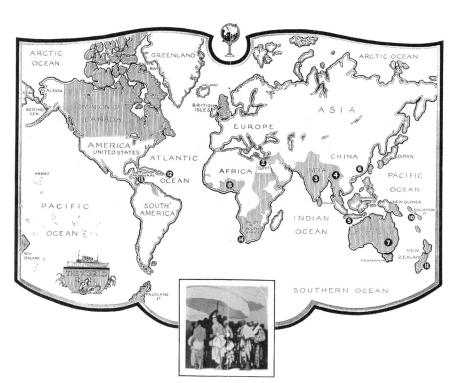

"MR. AUSTIN REED, I PRESUME."

The 'tonsorial Taj Mahal', the 34-chair barber's shop on the lower ground floor at Regent Street, opened in 1930. It still operates today, albeit with fewer chairs.

Another addition to the Regent Street store was a greatly expanded barber's shop, with baths, showers, and other facilities for the City man-about-town, all in the latest designs, including a serpentine neon light that circled the centre of the room – just another part of Austin Reed's top-to-toe service, which also included theatre tickets. Other barber's shops were installed in Austin Reed branches in Victoria Street, Fenchurch Street – members of Lloyd's were particular customers – Leeds, Norwich and Sheffield.

When the extension was completed it had increased effective floor-space in the Regent Street store by nearly 50 per cent.

Austin also began expanding his provincial network again with a shop in Donegall Place, Belfast, where the barber's shop became the unofficial meeting-place for the Northern Ireland Cabinet. 'With the development of Belfast as a governmental and administrative centre, the possibilities of trade should materially increase,' he told the share-holders optimistically, revealing another increase in profits to £85,000 during 1929. Austin Reed also bought a factory in Dalston Lane, Hack-ney, in which to manufacture shirts.

But 1930 was to prove less satisfactory. It was the year in which recession, signalled by the Wall Street crash the year before, began to bite the British retailer hard. Profits fell, in spite of the increase in the number of sales due to the new branches. The year after they fell again. 'Adverse trading conditions were more pronounced than in any previous period in the company's history,' Austin reported soberly. 'Falling prices combined with the greatly reduced spending-

The cutting room at the Dalston Lane shirt factory in Hackney, photographed in 1936. Note the patterns hanging from the work benches.

Modern Man was brought out by Austin Reed as a magazine for customers. It contained a mixture of advertisements, information, topical articles and helpful tips – everything required to make the readers feel well-informed gentlemen.

Modern Man

A MASCULINE MAGAZINE

MY EXQUISITE and sincere umbrella had gone. I stood there as pale as death. I did not raise unmanly cries, nor beat my breast, nor claw the ground. A man who is stricken with a sudden disaster, a man who has lost a great love, or a stud, or has fluffed a three-inch putt, or fallen off a house—such a man, if he is a man, bites on the bullet and is silent."

❖ ❖ ❖

THIS poignant passage from Mr. D. B. Wyndham Lewis expresses the sentiments—if not the practice—of most men. Times are hectic, but we must have fortitude. While it has become more and more simple to lose umbrellas, it has become more and more difficult to replace them. Better qualities are produced daily, but the eye of a specialist is needed to 'spot' their subtle superiorities. Every lost property office has its queue of baffled laymen trying to replace a lost umbrella with a better one.

❖ ❖ ❖

TO-DAY is the day of the specialist. The optimistic handyman who used to overhaul our car and cut our hair for an inclusive fee is gone. Nowadays we take our carburetter to a carburetter man, our magneto to a magneto man, and our hair to an artist who only handles heads of a certain social standing. *Modern Man*, being itself thoroughly modern, has decided to assume the air of a specialist. It has taken on the duties of a guide through the world of masculine accoutrements.

IN its search for authoritative contributors it has combed out London from the Athenæum to the National Sporting Club, and in the course of its survey has discovered quite a lot of gentlemen of wide experience and informative ability. This has been particularly so in the case of clothes, and incidentally it has discovered in this connection that, whereas many men profess to regard fashion as a public nuisance, most men worth the name have a wholesome respect for it and are fastidious about its observance.

THE need for up-to-date information on the subject has become very pressing during the past few years. Nature has been busy opening out new fields of adventure for our men, and each changed condition demands special garb. Flying, for example. Imagine the reaction of a shopkeeper thirty years ago towards anyone who had asked for the Flying Department! Yet to-day—

Customer: "Flying Department?"
Salesman: "Yes, sir: second on the right, and take lift to the third floor, sir."

HERE is an obvious opportunity for *Modern Man*. It may not be necessary to advise removal of spurs before ascent, or warn a neophyte against sky-blue ties, but there are many details about which such a paper can be of great value. The number of privately-owned machines is steadily increasing, and as more and more men take to flight, more and more brains will be busily engaged in devising more suitable equipment. Change will follow change in quick succession, and *Modern Man* will be ready to mark the evolution and pass on the information to its readers.

❖ ❖ ❖

FLYING may seem rather an extreme example, but the same sort of thing is happening in a minor key in every other branch of masculine activity. Take golf. Speaking generally, the ordinary golfer does not realise how much the clothes affect the man. Few of them are aware of the untiring effort made by manufacturers and designers in their search for perfection in shoes, stockings, and every other garment, in order to add to a man's comfort and efficiency in a round of golf.

❖ ❖ ❖

BARELY a week passes without the birth of some new idea whereby improvement is effected in men's clothes. Wherever these developments are born, there you will find *Modern Man* in attendance, carefully collecting information and ideas—looking down the chimney, listening at the keyhole, periscoping from the basement.

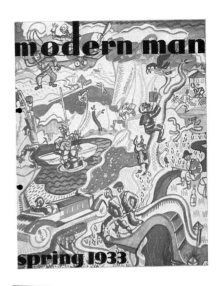

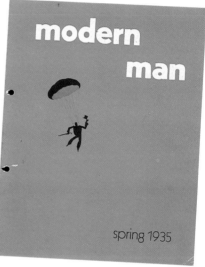

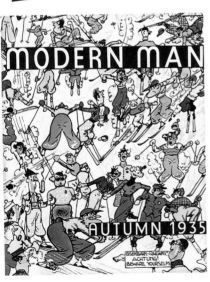

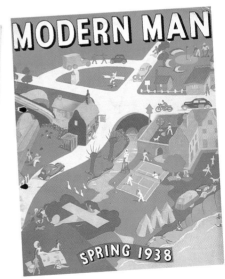

Douglas Austin Reed, photographed shortly before his marriage to Mary Philpott on 12 July 1930.

The AR brand names begin to appear abroad.

Summit
DRESS WEAR
at Mackintosh's

power of the community to which your company more particularly makes its appeal, have been the two main causes. Other contributing causes have been the marked decrease in the number of overseas visitors and the very unseasonable weather experienced, especially during the summer months.'

The only bright spot from Austin's point of view was the fact that his elder son Douglas had been appointed a director after six years with the company. Douglas, then in his late twenties, had largely overcome a youthful stammer which had contributed to an appearance of diffidence that concealed a wicked sense of humour. He went to Mill Hill School and joined Austin Reed in 1926 after training with suppliers and other retailers in Britain and the US. Initially he was in the buying department with Deane and Bone, becoming particularly knowledgeable about neckwear. From about 1930 he was instrumental in developing an international network of retail agents for Summit shirts and collars, including Meddens in Holland, Ströms in Sweden, Brødrene Andersen in Denmark, Ferner Jacobsen in Norway, Hugh Wright in New Zealand, Wardrop in Australia, and Mackintosh in Hong Kong. The sons of many of these retailers came to Austin Reed for training.

This involved Douglas travelling regularly around Scandinavia and Europe. (He usually managed to stop off at St Moritz in the winter to bobsleigh on the Cresta Run.) As a result of these overseas connections, well-known personalities such as Robert Menzies, Pandit Nehru, and Jomo Kenyatta first heard of Austin Reed. This export department also became the forerunner of Austin Reed International.

Douglas's opposite number in the buying department, incidentally, was his sister Phyllis's husband, Kenneth Tremellen, who looked after the hosiery. Another son-in-law, Robert (Bertie) Robertson, who was married to Austin's eldest daughter, Stella, had joined the company in 1930. Both Tremellen and Robertson later became directors.

Flög över Atlanten
och köpte Austin Reed-skjortor!

Kurt Björkvall ekiperade sig från topp till tå i Austin Reed's affär på Regent Str.

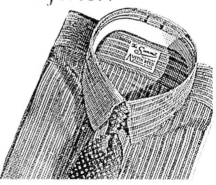

STRÖMS
REGERINGSGATAN 19-21

Douglas was not the first new director. Since 1926 Eric Collins had been on the board. Collins's elder brother had been Austin's best man and had married one of Emily's sisters. Eric went to South Africa as a young man and worked in the Kimberley diamond-fields, before serving with the South African forces in the First World War. He had been chosen by Austin and Percy Osborn to run the new Regent Street store and he had made a directorship a condition.

Douglas's appointment was followed three years later by more promotions to the board: Claude Hills, in reward for his achievements with the New Tailoring, and Bob Shorter, the long-serving display manager. By then the business was looking up again, with profits back to the 1928 level and further branches opening in the Corn Exchange, Manchester, London Wall, Oxford, and Norwich, while the Regent Street store had grown again to take in premises in Vigo Street.

The improvements in results also gave Austin the opportunity to start a staff pension scheme at a cost of £36,000. Staff contributions would be 4 per cent of their salaries, with the company making an equal donation.

Another fillip to the regional chain came in 1936 with the take-over of Walter Scott Menswear, which had branches in Nottingham, Hull, Coventry, Southampton, and Plymouth. The shops were fitted out well enough to integrate directly into the group, but the stock had to be changed. Austin Reed also bought a fine site in Princes Street, Edinburgh, but that had to be entirely refitted. Despite bad weather, and an unsettled economy, profits were nearly up to the record level of 1929, but they did not reflect the real growth in Austin Reed, which was close to becoming a national chain.

Douglas Reed, rear man on the bobsleigh, shooting down the Cresta Run.

6

'Just a Part of the Austin Reed Service'

By the 1930s 'It's just a part of the Austin Reed service' had become a national catch-phrase, used by all sorts of people who had nothing to do with the company. This was largely due to the national success of Austin Reed's advertising, particularly the Fougasse cartoons. But it would not have carried conviction without an underlying truth. There really was a special quality of service in all Austin Reed branches, with the staff patently eager to help and proud of the quality of the goods they were selling. This in turn reflected two fundamental influences. One was Austin's unflagging commitment to service as an ideal. And the other was the very personal hands-on approach of his senior management, still headed by Albert Deane and Percy Osborn.

Philip Horton was one month short of his eighteenth birthday when he began working for Austin Reed in the company's Fenchurch Street branch. The date was 1 May 1923 and the City shop was still the company's flagship. He had applied for a job at Austin Reed's because his father knew a man who knew Percy Osborn. Horton himself, then in his last term at Watford Grammar School, had little idea of what he wanted to do, which made him typical of half the young men who ended up in the retail menswear trade. The other half tended to have family connections in the rag trade.

Osborn greeted the tall, skinny youth with a smile, quizzed him briefly and asked him when he would like to start. Both the smile and the swift offer of employment were untypical. Osborn's usual demeanour was far less friendly and most applicants were told that there was a waiting-list for jobs in Austin Reed, which in any case only employed people of exceptional talent. Neither statement, in fact, was entirely true. Austin Reed's expansion meant that the company was constantly in need of staff, while the work itself, with its long hours and simple and repetitive tasks, did not require especially high levels of education or intellect. What were required, however, were

Above: A cartoon from a 1930s *Modern Man.*

Opposite: Tom Purvis's inimitable style became synonymous with Austin Reed quality.

67

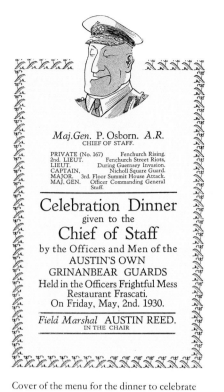

Maj.Gen. P. Osborn. *A.R.*
CHIEF OF STAFF.

PRIVATE (No. 167)   Fenchurch Rising.
2nd. LIEUT.   Fenchurch Street Riots.
LIEUT.   During Guernsey Invasion.
CAPTAIN.   Nicholl Square Guard.
MAJOR.   3rd. Floor Summit House Attack.
MAJ. GEN. Officer Commanding General Staff.

Celebration Dinner
given to the
Chief of Staff
by the Officers and Men of the
AUSTIN'S OWN
GRINANBEAR GUARDS
Held in the Officers Frightful Mess
Restaurant Frascati.
On Friday, May, 2nd. 1930.

Field Marshal AUSTIN REED.
IN THE CHAIR

Cover of the menu for the dinner to celebrate Percy Osborn's twenty-fifth year with the company.

A touch of humour from a staff pension booklet of the 1930s.

"The commencing salary is only fifteen shillings, but you get a pension at sixty."

cheerfulness, resilience, honesty and natural good manners. Intentionally or not, Osborn had evolved interviewing techniques which tested for these qualities by putting candidates under severe pressure. How much this was a reflection of his real nature was hard to decide. Off duty, or among his peers, he was pleasant enough. As staff director, though, he exercised an extraordinary ability to strike fear into Austin Reed's junior employees.

Expectations in the 1920s were modest, however, and most young men were only too pleased to obtain work at any price. Habits of deference were also deeply ingrained, so such brusqueness was endured and all but expected.

By the time Philip Horton came seeking a job, too, the standards of customer service at Austin Reed had become well known in the retail trade, so Osborn could justify the obstacle course he erected in front of would-be employees as a method of discovering the 'right stuff'. His aggression flushed out any tendency to answer back, while the waiting-list discouraged the faint-hearted. Philip Horton, it would appear, was lucky. Obviously the friend of the family really did know Osborn – who, however, could not forgo the chance of playing at least one of his exploitative tricks. 'Can you start on May the first?' he asked Horton innocently. 'Certainly,' said the young man agreeably, although he could easily have begun as soon as he left school. When in due course he arrived for his first day, resplendent in stiff white collar, white shirt, studs and cuff-links, dark serge suit, and shiny black shoes, his discreetly oiled hair brushed severely back under a brand new straw hat, Horton's new colleagues greeted him with knowing smiles. 'Do you know why you have begun on May the first?' they asked. He confessed the date had been suggested by Mr Osborn. They laughed unkindly. 'Because anyone who starts on or after the first of May gets no holiday this year!'

Horton realized that he had entered a new and hard world. His hours were 8.50 a.m. to 6.30 p.m. during the week and 1.30 p.m. on Saturdays. Including commuting to Watford, this made a 70-hour week, for which his net pay was only 9s. 2d. before rail fares and lunches. The first six months were a salutary introduction to the delights of adulthood. Once this trial period was over, however, his pay was doubled to £1 gross – still not a great sum but infinitely preferable to the unemployment that was beginning to stalk so many.

As time went by, Horton began to enjoy his work. Fenchurch Street had just been refurbished by Westwood, inspired by his American trip, with handsome display units in which the goods were displayed in trays behind glass slides. The floors were polished wood, while a spacious flight of stairs took customers to the upper and lower floors. Concealed lighting and central-heating made the shop a pleasant environment in which to work, while Horton found he enjoyed selling

to customers who obviously appreciated both the goods and the attention Austin Reed lavished on them.

Much of the work, admittedly, was labour-intensive. Most of the goods taken out of the display cabinets for inspection had to be refolded and replaced – and, in the case of underwear, repacked in either threes or sixes in whitish paper done up with string. If the customer bought something his purchase was also tied with string in green paper neatly torn from rolls of varying widths.

Then there was the endless chore of keeping stock and sale records. By the 1920s Austin had stopped paying commission because he felt it encouraged employees to oversell, which he believed deterred customers from returning as well as discouraging staff from spending time on goodwill exercises such as dealing with complaints or giving advice. Instead he had instituted a bonus system, which gave everyone in a branch a reward based on total takings over a period.

All staff had to be punctilious about stock control and pricing.

Just a part of the Austin Reed service available at Regent Street.

The ground floor of the New Street, Birmingham, shop shows the Bauhaus influence on the 1930s interior.

Horton had, for example, to learn the 'code', a group of letters which disguised the wholesale price from customers. In Austin Reed's shops this was based on the word CUMBERLAND, with C standing for 1, U for 2 and so on until N for 9 and D for zero, plus H for a repeated number. So BH, for example, stood for 44. Compared to some businesses, it was simple enough. Horton was completely baffled by the code adopted by one of Austin's suppliers, the hosiery company I. & R. Morley, which used the letters RLEPTMDOXFH. They stood, he eventually discovered, for the words: 'Remember Lord every prayer that Morley doth offer except for himself.'

If a branch lacked an item requested by a customer, Horton learned to use Austin Reed's internal telephone system to ring round other branches to ask if any of them could supply it. If he was lucky, it would be put on one of the firm's delivery-vans and delivered within an hour. But every item had to be recorded on inter-branch records so the stock total could be adjusted at both branches. Woe betide the branch that let a customer go away unsatisfied without recording the fact. Each shop had a 'swap book' in which any shortage of stock had to be recorded, even if it was something Austin Reed did not sell.

The branches would, in fact, happily take orders from customers for products or sizes they did not normally keep. As the junior, Horton was frequently dispatched to 'do' the City, which meant walking to Wood Street to call on some of the wholesalers with which Austin Reed dealt, such as Morley, Aertex, William Hollins for Viyella, and Ricks or Sambrook Whitting for ties. Shirts came from the Hammersmith factory of Bryce & Weston, far enough away to justify using a van.

All stock had to be recorded, for that matter, which meant another code to add to every invoice. Again this code was alphabetical and it soon became branded on Horton's memory. Even in his eighties he could recall it without effort. A for clothing, B for goods made to special order, C for ties, D for gloves, E for hairdressing, F for collars, G for shirts, H for hosiery, J for jewellery, K for handkerchiefs, L for braces and suspenders, M for woollens and pullovers, N for pyjamas, O for fancy, P for boots and shoes, Q for theatre tickets, R for posting, packaging, and insurance, S for tobacco, T for hats, U for underwear, V for valeting, W for walking-sticks, X for tropical, Y for luggage, and Z for washing, cleaning, and redressing.

All the details were also punched into a Powers Samas card index, so that Austin Reed had a total overview of its stock by item, branch, and value with the previous week's sales' figures arriving on Tuesday afternoon. It enabled the company to check on pilfering, and was essential to the twice-a-year stocktaking – conducted on the first occasion by the manager of each branch and the second time by a manager from another branch, to make sure corruption was not taking place from

One of many booklets produced to help and inform customers. 'To clothe the man with the major elegance and the minor nicety . . . to maintain essential standards in the most informal wear . . . to bring comfort to the most precise tailoring . . . is just a part of the Austin Reed Service.'

Opposite: Another innovative AR service was to sell '"Dress Garments" as opposed to "Dress Suits", and, all garments being made from the same cloth, men could always replace an individual garment and be sure that the two parts of the suit would match.'

The annual branch trophy was introduced in 1935, and is still competed for today. Its streamlined shape was designed by Raymond McGrath, who also designed the Schneider aviation trophy.

A page from the Austin Reed 'Community Songs' book, which was used at special staff 'smokers', and the front cover of the first copy of *The Tie*, launched in 1920.

A.R. COMMUNITY SONGS.

5

Tune—

" Clementine,"

Hear our voicing song rejoicing
To the name of Austin Reed's,
Where discerning men go yearning
For their shirts and all their needs.

Chorus. Loudly singing, welkins ringing,
We proclaim afar in rhyme
An unbroken worthy slogan,
Service first, and all the time.

The TIE A 'get-together' MAGAZINE

the top. Not that there was much chance of that; not while Osborn was in charge. He was constantly calling on branches and subjecting them to an inspection that any sergeant-major would have respected.

Like the ex-soldiers that so many of them were, the staff learned to anticipate his demands and his movements. The first line of defence was a phone call from Gwladys Jones (later to become the second Mrs Eric Collins) at head office, who could be trusted to provide the confidential information that 'Ozzie' was on his way, giving the branch time to tidy up and stand by its counters.

The bolder also discovered that Osborn respected people who stood up to him. Horton earned his spurs when he politely insisted that the staff director approve the tidiness of a storeroom that he had castigated on a previous visit. Osborn gave Horton a thunderous look, inspected the room without comment, and then asked him to lunch at the Strand Palace Hotel, where he assuaged his feelings by bullying the waiter. Horton, however, never received a harsh word from him again.

This did not mean that Osborn relaxed his unbending standards, although it was on an earlier occasion that Horton asked him for an increase in salary. 'And why, pray?' Horton muttered something about thinking that he did his job well. 'Of course you do your job well. You wouldn't be here if you didn't. We don't give salary increases for doing your job; we give salary increases for doing more than your job!' As a statement of the Austin Reed creed, the words were remarkably close to the truth. Employees really were expected to contribute more than the call of duty might dictate. They were proud to work for Austin Reed, weren't they? The surprising thing was that they were proud; very proud. When it came to men's retailing, they had no doubt at all that they were privileged to work for the very best company of all. The reason was not hard to find. If Percy Osborn was the stick, Austin Reed was the carrot. He loved his company, cherished its reputation, and devoted himself to its well-being.

Austin was an unabashed paternalist who had no inhibitions about imposing his own beliefs on his employees, and demanding from them standards of performance every bit as high as his own. Unlike Osborn, however, he was a persuader rather than a driver. He liked to lead from the front, a technique which meant being visible at all times. He enjoyed being with his colleagues and encouraged the growth of social activities of all kinds. In the early days cementing staff relations required no more than annual staff outings and dinners, but by the 1920s Austin Reed's staff activities were becoming more formal, with a sports club and a dramatic society, plus a modest house magazine called *The Tie*.

A small leaflet with a buff cover and an old-fashioned type-face, *The Tie* was as much a propaganda medium as a vehicle for staff news and views. It provided Austin and his senior colleagues with an extended

72

notice-board on which to continue the education of their growing workforce whom, inevitably, they knew less and less intimately.

Some of their homilies were direct: 'May I stress, through the columns of *The Tie*, the absolute necessity for all members of Sales Staff not only to read, but thoroughly to digest our weekly advertising ... Two of the essentials to successful salesmanship can be supplied in a large measure by careful and intelligent reading of our weekly shop advertising. One is the necessity of finding points of contact with your customer and the other is an intimate knowledge of the goods you are selling.'

Or: 'Can you tell the size your customer takes in collars, gloves, and socks at a glance? I know this comes by experience, but have you made a definite mental effort to become proficient in this direction? Do you know offhand the relative value of centimetres and inches for the benefit of foreign customers?'

Others were less specific, but still promoted qualities of salesmanship and service, from an article about starting work at Austin Reed to information about the size of various customer markets. Coupled with day-to-day supervision and encouragement, the propaganda worked. Not all Austin Reed's employees threw themselves into their jobs with fervour, but many were eager to play their part in sustaining the company's reputation for exceptional service.

Occasionally, it took some living up to. Some customers apparently credited Austin Reed with psychic powers. One telephoned with a demand for a selection of shirts to be delivered immediately to his address. Asked the size, he replied simply 'I am tall and broad. Hurry up!'

AR kept all their overseas customers' English addresses on file. This service could be very useful. On one occasion two golfers who met on the boat from India lost contact, but as both visited the tropical department and mentioned the matter, AR were able to put them in touch again.

Austin with the staff council in 1934. It was formed in the 1920s to discuss the day-to-day running of the company, and make recommendations.

FOUR FLOORS NOW

SEE MAP

EMPIRE LINEN

a new kind of summer underwear

It's just a part of the Austin Reed service

100 IDEAS for PRESENTS for MEN

as a matter of fact

DRESS CLOTHES

EVENING WEAR

Austin Reed of REGENT STREET London

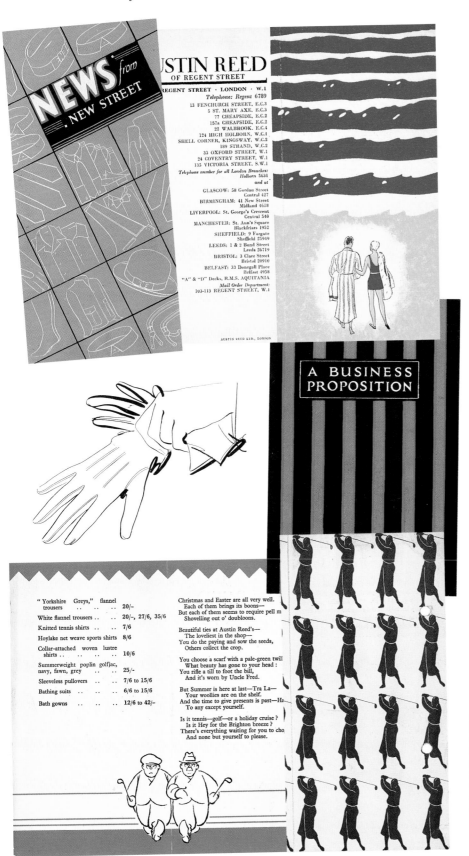

Austin Reed produced a variety of different booklets on all sorts of subjects. Some were more directly sales oriented than others – for example, the '100 Ideas for Presents for Men' contains a list of goods available at Austin Reed and their prices, whereas the 'How to Get Married' booklet is a humorous guide to etiquette and – most important – who pays for what. Right at the end are two pages headed 'Our Contribution', advertising the New Tailoring at Austin Reed to fill all the prospective bridegroom's needs.

Sea Island Shirts

Nowhere in the world is there a better shirt than this Summit Shirt made from Sea Island Cotton. British throughout, it is cut in coat-style, with mother-of-pearl buttons. There are two sleeve lengths. Two cutaway collars which allow ample space for the tie are included. You may choose from numerous stripe designs.

Price 63/-

AUSTIN REED *of Regent Street*

LONDON AND PRINCIPAL CITIES · LONDON TELEPHONE : REGENT 6789

Right: Austin (left) and Sir Philip Cunliffe-Lister, Secretary of State for the Colonies, later the Earl of Swinton, at the opening of the Sea Island Cotton promotion in Regent Street in May 1935, and *above* an advertisement for Sea Island shirts. The company did much to promote this fine shirting fabric, benefiting the economies of St Lucia and other West Indian islands.

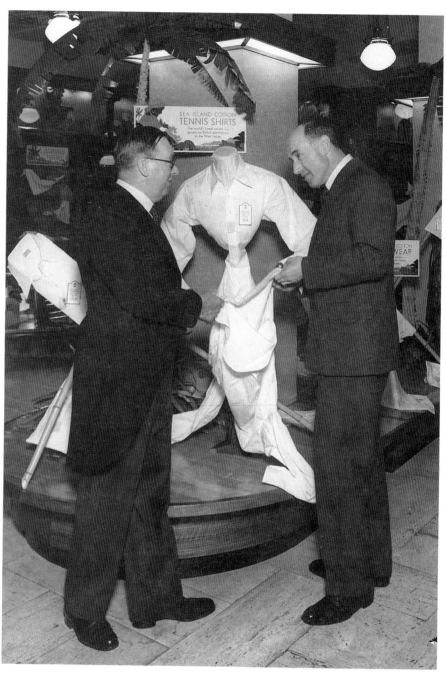

A request to supply the opera star Gigli with a grey top-hat in his suite at the Savoy was complicated by the singer's refusal to answer queries about whether it fitted, because he had been ordered to rest his voice. And a delivery to the Prime Minister, Ramsay MacDonald, at No. 10 Downing Street was delayed when the salesman was mistaken by press photographers for the future president of the Irish Republic, Éamon de Valera.

Others were more specific but equally demanding. Just after the Second World War, for example, Sir Arthur 'Bomber' Harris, commander-in-chief of Bomber Command, rang at 4 p.m. one afternoon to demand a white waistcoat and evening-shirt for a 52-inch chest, a 19½-inch collar, two white ties, and a pair of white gloves at the Park Lane Hotel by 3 p.m. the next day. Overnight Austin Reed had the ties handmade in Richmond and the shirts tailored in its Dalston workshop. The waistcoat, collar, and gloves were in stock.

Predictably, some customers tried to exploit the company's commitment to service. Most frequent was the return of items which had clearly been damaged by careless wear or washing. As a matter of policy, Austin Reed always took them back, although it became adept at making clear to customers that it had seen through them. The danger of fraud was always present, and Austin Reed's policy of refusing cheques from anyone unknown to the company remained firmly in place. But it was not always easy to enforce, as in the case of the enormous black man who arrived at Regent Street in a vast Rolls-Royce. Escorted round the store, he selected a large number of items, asked to pay by cheque and presented a card which said simply 'Black Eagle, Gun Runner'. The manager decided discretion was the better part of valour, but sent an assistant out for a quiet word with the chauffeur of the car. Yes, the driver said, it did belong to Mr Black Eagle, and what's more it was the only Rolls-Royce ever made with a lavatory in the back seat.

151 FITTINGS AND VARIATIONS IN THE

NEW TAILORING

This stylish advertisement appeared in the 1930s. 'It is an interesting fact that . . . the majority of women agree with the majority of men that a man's clothes should be seen and not heard.'

R.M.S. "Queen Mary"

R.M.S. "Queen Elizabeth"

7

Down to
the Sea in Shops

T H E opportunity to operate a branch of Austin Reed on the transatlantic liner *Aquitania* came in 1929. Cunard's decision to offer the franchise to Austin Reed reflected the extent to which the company had established itself as the premier menswear retailer in the UK.

Austin's motives for accepting the challenge were just as clear. He saw it as a wonderful chance to promote his company's name to the world's élite. The first-class passenger list on the six-day crossing aboard the luxury Cunarder was a cross-section of the richest and most famous people in Europe and the United States, and the cabin-class accommodation was filled with affluent travellers for whom Austin Reed would be a first taste of Britain.

Two shops were fitted out in three-day bursts during the Cunarder's Southampton turnaround by Percy Westwood, whose austere, beautifully crafted shop units, with their fine woods and precisely made sliding shelves and doors, could have been designed for a ship in the first place. They were opened on 29 June 1929 by the Mayor of Southampton, who marked the occasion by buying two identical hand-woven silk ties made in Spitalfields, one for himself and one to be presented to the Mayor of New York in six days' time with the message 'a bit of Regent Street'. As well as selling clothes, the shop also offered a booking-service for such first-class necessities as London theatres, fishing on the Wye, or private aeroplanes. The innovation was widely reported in British newspapers and magazines.

The shop was staffed on its maiden crossing by Austin Reed salesmen from Regent Street and Victoria Street and by Donald McCullough, the company's advertising and press relations manager. The weather was fine and the trip uneventful, with American passengers most impressed by the modesty of Austin Reed's prices.

The arrival in New York was the opportunity for another press conference and photocall, at which the Mayor of New York made a

Above: 'Before you weigh anchor we invite you to Austin Reed's. We will then gladly talk over this whole cruising business with you and see that you have all you need without it costing you an unnecessary penny.'

Opposite: Paintings of the Queens from menus used on board. In between is an AR booklet, 'It may surprise you to know . . .'

Donald McCullough (*right*) makes a presentation from the Mayor of Southampton to Jimmy Walker, Mayor of New York, in 1929.

generous speech of welcome. McCullough then nervously presented the gift from his counterpart in Southampton. The Mayor, expecting perhaps a case of whisky, expressed his thanks courteously but mutedly. Press comment in the USA was equally reserved.

Austin staffed the shops economically with one senior salesman and two assistants. Being seconded to the *Aquitania* was real adventure. It began with a train journey from Waterloo to Southampton on a Monday afternoon and two nights in the Crown Hotel. Tuesday was spent in the docks, locating the crates of new stock that had been sent down from London to replenish the shops after the previous crossing and carrying them down the ship's apparently endless supply-corridor to Austin Reed's storage rooms on U deck, only just over the bilges. All the merchandise was under seal so none could be unpacked until after the vessel sailed at midday on Wednesday, first to anchor off Cherbourg to pick up Continental passengers from a tender and then out past the Bishop Rock and into the Atlantic.

The first-class shop was well placed on A Deck to catch passing trade. It faced what was called the Long Gallery, a sweeping promenade with large windows facing the sea all along one side. Tables and chairs at which waiters served passengers with drinks, morning coffee, and afternoon tea, were scattered down its length, and the gallery also served as a miniature street down which people could stroll and, of course, spend.

Apart from the chore of collecting replacement stock from the bowels of the *Aquitania*, working conditions for Austin Reed's seafaring staff were markedly better than on land. The economy of staff meant that assistants were relatively unsupervised and, as the shops only opened between 10 a.m. and 5 p.m. with an hour off at lunchtimes, their hours were much shorter.

For the remainder of the voyage the young men were treated as cabin-class passengers. This was another benefit of Austin's decision to rotate his shipboard staff. Permanent employees, such as hairdressers, travelled on ship's papers, which made them *de facto* members of the crew. Austin Reed's part-timers travelled on their own passports,

RMS *Aquitania* entering Southampton Water.

sharing a cabin in the cabin-class section. To preserve their status, Austin Reed subsidized the payment of tips to the stewards and a special sweetener for the lift-man, to prevent him complaining about the continual traffic of merchandise from U deck.

The rest was paradise. Especially the food. Early morning tea was followed by a full English breakfast, with a nourishing cup of soup at 11 a.m. and a three- or four-course luncheon. Tea and cucumber sandwiches relieved the pangs of hunger at about 3.30 p.m., after which there was nothing until dinner at 7 p.m. Finally more sandwiches were available late in the evening, with a large bowl of fruit always in the cabin to stave off night starvation. Austin Reed's staff, their youthful appetites sharpened by sea air, rose manfully to the challenge. They also enjoyed the social life on board ship, revelling in their egalitarian treatment by American passengers.

The *Aquitania* provided its passengers with a leisurely itinerary. As well as taking six days to cross the Atlantic, she spent another five or six days in port, a lie-over which gave Austin Reed's employees plenty of time to see the sights in New York. Add Cunard's intermittent cruises and a young Austin Reed salesman could easily spend a month away from home.

The cruises were the result of prohibition. When the shops first opened on the *Aquitania*, the US was only just slipping into the Great Depression, but it had already made alcohol illegal in most states. One of the great attractions of foreign liners was their freedom from the ban on drink. Cunard was quick to cash in on American deprivation by interspersing its transatlantic service with short 'booze cruises' to Canada or the Bahamas. The instant the *Aquitania* crossed the three-mile limit all its bars snapped open for as long as the voyage lasted, which was up to fourteen days, providing scope for some monumental binges.

Willy-nilly Austin Reed's young men went along for the ride, which could be wild. The *Aquitania*'s North American passengers unbuttoned under the benign protection of the Cunard flag with intense enthusiasm. Once they had taken the edge off their thirst they looked eagerly for other ways to spend their money. Among the beneficiaries were Austin Reed's branches, which hastened to capitalize on the demand, even to the extent of opening in the evenings. The rewards could be rich, if surprising. One evening, for example, a somewhat high-flown passenger, attracted by a pair of red silk pyjamas in the window, bought them and put them on over his evening clothes, to the hilarity of his companions. The next morning one of the *Aquitania*'s cleaners found the pyjamas behind a chair in the Long Gallery; they were never reclaimed. Presumably to the purchaser their expensive price was worth the thirty seconds' laughter they provoked, assuming he remembered the incident at all.

Stanley Reed (left) and Doug Davis relaxing between shop opening hours on board the *Aquitania*. Austin's younger brother had led a fairly chequered career since his Oxford Street days.

81

EFFICIENT LUGGAGE

AUSTIN REED LTD

A display showing the Austin Reed range of luggage suitable to take on board ship.

The Duke of Windsor *en route* to New York.

In 1936, the company was given a concession on the *Queen Mary*, and there were also two Austin Reed Shops on the *Queen Elizabeth* when she, too, came into passenger service ten years later. These two great ships, the *Queen Mary* and the *Queen Elizabeth*, kept up a regular schedule, criss-crossing the Atlantic in a little over four days.

As each voyage progressed, a very high proportion of the passengers visited the Austin Reed shops. Many were rich or famous. Some bought, but others were just there to browse or even to chat. Austin Reed's staff, trained to courtesy under the severest provocation, sometimes found themselves fulfilling a social role outside their previous experience. The ultimate test was perhaps the quiet afternoon the Duke of Windsor wandered in to the first-class shop on the *Queen Elizabeth*, ostensibly to inspect Austin Reed's wares. 'Do you get tea here?' he queried hesitantly. 'Of course, sir,' said Austin Reed's young gentleman and hastened to summon a waiter. And the ex-King sat beside the counter in Austin Reed's shop and sipped tea and asked rather sadly about everyday life in England. This encounter took place on the maiden voyage of the *Queen Elizabeth* as a passenger ship.

As the Second World War drew nearer, an increasing number of third- or tourist-class passengers were refugees from Hitler's Europe. In almost every case they had been prevented by the Nazis from taking any money out of Germany, so Cunard issued each of them with a small number of vouchers, worth about 5s. each, to pay for necessary items on board ship. Many refugees, however, were so desperate for money to spend in New York that they preferred to go without. The only problem was converting the vouchers into cash. A favourite solution was to buy the cheapest item possible, for example a bar of chocolate costing 2*d.*, and pocket the change. All Austin Reed's staff could offer these poor people was sympathy.

Shortly before Britain declared war on Germany the *Queen Mary* began her last commercial crossing to New York with the largest number of passengers ever carried across the Atlantic at one time. Austin Reed had stocked its shops as normal, but few of the refugees on board were in a position to buy. As the ship approached New York the Captain announced that war had been declared that day. Two days after docking Victor Short, who was in charge of Austin Reed's shops for the voyage, discovered that the *Queen Mary* was staying in America, but the crew was to sail for England next day on another ship. He immediately told the chief purser that he had no intention of abandoning Austin Reed's valuable stock. He cabled London for instructions and was told to try and sell everything in New York. This proved easier said than done, apart from cashmere knitwear, and after some days, Short and his colleagues locked everything away in a steel stockroom alongside the second-class swimming-pool and sailed home in the *Manhattan*.

This 1930s AR poster could be seen on Waterloo station by passengers catching the boat train to Southampton *en route* to America.

The exterior of the Austin Reed shop in first-class on board the *Queen Mary*.

Inside the first-class shop on the *Queen Mary*.
The beautiful wooden interiors were designed
by Percy Westwood in true shipboard style,
and the fixtures constructed to keep the stock
secure in rough weather.

One of several booklets produced by Austin
Reed as a guide to nautical dos and don'ts, this
is 'Sea Legs: A Complete Guide to Cruising'.

Eventually, however, Austin sold the surplus stock to Filene's Automatic Bargain Basement in Boston, which promptly advertised the coup in lavish terms:

$26,312 stock now $11,320. Luxury values to your Bond Street taste at Filene's Basement famous giveaway low prices (for Christmas gifts) the most sensational purchase we've stumbled across in all our 31 years of bargain history. Highlights: Sea Island cotton shirts – tropical hats – men's foulard shirts – English tweed caps – Indian cashmere sweaters – soft rich wool lounging-robes – women's fine Braemar cashmere sweaters. Note: the *Queen Mary* tie, especially designed for the *Queen Mary* by Austin Reed with official approval of the Cunard White Star Lines. The narrow line of royal purple symbolizes the launching of the *Queen Mary* and the active interest shown by the Royal Family.

The *Queen Elizabeth* made her first commercial voyage in the autumn of 1946, with Harry Tee as Austin Reed's shipboard manager and Jack Hutchens from Regent Street and Ralph Cook from Liverpool manning the shops filled with £17,000-worth of stock, worth approximately £250,000 at 1990 prices. The shops were besieged by customers immediately the ship sailed, to the particular alarm of the bodyguards attending the Russian Foreign Minister, Vyacheslav Molotov, whose stateroom was next to the branch on the Main Deck. The press only slackened at dinner-time and it took Austin Reed's staff until two in the morning to restock. When Tee arrived next morning, he found queues already waiting. Wisely, he kept the doors firmly closed, only letting two or three customers in at a time. The queues remained undiminished for as long as the shops stayed open.

There was a period during which the shipboard shops made more money than any Austin Reed branch on land with the exception of Regent Street. There were severe shortages of every kind in the UK and clothes rationing was rigidly enforced. Shipboard stock, however, was exempt. The Austin Reed shops seized the opportunity to carry a comprehensive range of 'export only' menswear. As soon as a ship left Southampton, a queue of outward-bound British customers would form which sometimes seemed to last for the best part of 3,000 miles. On arrival in New York, a cable would be sent to the London stock-room detailing the amount sold, so that a van could be waiting with replacement merchandise on the return to England.

Business was not quite as brisk on the way back, with British passengers replaced by American visitors alert to the opportunity to buy presents for their UK hosts. As always, many were famous as well as rich. Under the pressure of coping with demand, Austin Reed's staff did not always have time to recognize celebrity. One particularly busy

Outside the first-class shop on the *Queen Elizabeth.*

Above: Douglas Fairbanks, one of Austin Reed's more famous customers, lends a knee to Mary Pickford on arriving in Southampton.

Above right: A collection of customers' signatures from the visitors' book kept in the first-class shops on the ships.

morning on board the *Queen Elizabeth* a young woman with striking red hair eased her way to the counter and asked for a red cashmere sweater. 'Would it help if I sorted one out for myself?' she said sympathetically to the embattled assistant. She looked through the shelves and removed every red sweater in stock. 'I'll take them all,' she said. 'They are all different sizes, miss,' the assistant said anxiously. 'Don't worry, so are my friends.' 'I'm afraid I can't wrap them up for you just now,' the assistant apologized. 'That's all right. My word, you are busy. Would you like some help?' 'Well, thank you very much, miss.' And for the next half-hour the unpaid junior sales assistant in Austin Reed's shop on the *Queen Elizabeth* was the film star Maureen O'Sullivan, a fact which did nothing to shorten the queue of customers. Some film stars, of course, were unmistakable. Gary Cooper, for example, owes Ralph Cook a dime to this day.

In the post-war years the pressure of competition from airlines began to cut into the profitability of the liners, which responded by increasing the frequency of their voyages and making ever-more desperate efforts

'Fantasy' by Fougasse.

to woo passengers. Gradually the *Queens* turned more and more to cruising and the profitability of Austin Reed's shops, as well as the ships themselves, began to fall away. By the early 1960s Austin Reed reluctantly accepted that the shipboard shops were no longer economic.

From a commercial point of view, in fact, they had only been really profitable for the few years after the Second World War. But as a means of publicizing the Austin Reed name, especially in the United States, they had been a magnificent success.

Cary Grant, another shipboard customer, photographed with an old friend on the *Queen Elizabeth* in 1947.

Some famous shipboard customers:

The Duke and Duchess of Windsor
Phyllis Calvert
Rex Harrison
The Prince of Tonga
R. A. Butler
Michael Wilding
King Peter of Yugoslavia
Arthur Rubinstein
Gracie Fields
Glynis Johns
Prince Monolulu
Peter Sellers
Fred Perry
Phil Silvers
Geraldo
Douglas Fairbanks
Lady Astor
John Mills
Marquess of Queensbury
Axel, Prince of Denmark
Elizabeth Taylor
Jerry Lewis
J. Arthur Rank
Henry Cotton
Winston Churchill
Lord Beaverbrook
Myrna Loy
Deborah Kerr
Lord Boothby
Duke of Bedford
T. O. M. Sopwith
Beverley Nichols
Admiral Lord Beatty
Cary Grant
Paulette Goddard
Alexander of Tunis
Stirling Moss

Lord Jellicoe
Jack Benny
Gregory Peck
Cecil Beaton
Pearl Bailey
Alec Guinness
Terence Rattigan
Spencer Tracy
Ralph Richardson
Charles Boyer
Randolph Churchill
Rita Hayworth
David Niven
Richard Burton
Dean Martin
Anthony Eden
Eleanor Roosevelt
Max Factor
Eamon Andrews
Bette Davis
Alan Ladd
Montgomery of Alamein
Yehudi Menuhin
Hannen Swaffer
Stan Laurel
Ernest Bevin
Gary Cooper
Richard Tauber

Modern Man

8

'Men Before Money': the Second World War

T HE declaration of war in 1939 was a great sorrow to Austin for more than one reason. To begin with, it meant abandoning any plans to retire. He was 66 and was ready to take life a little easier. In any case the old order was passing; Albert Deane and Percy Osborn had already resigned from the board two years earlier due to indifferent health and advancing years, and day-to-day management of the group had passed to Eric Collins, whom Austin had made joint managing director at the beginning of 1938. It was only a matter of time before Austin relinquished all formal executive power, although no one had any illusions that his interest in the company would diminish.

The start of the war, however, meant that any such development would have to be deferred. Once again the young men in Austin Reed hurried to enlist in the defence of their country, including Douglas's younger brother Kenneth. Born in 1917, Kenneth Reed was the youngest of Austin and Emily's six children (two boys, four girls). Educated at Oundle School and University College, Oxford, where he learnt to fly in the University Air Squadron, he worked for a short time at Red Lion Square in 1939 before enlisting and being commissioned in the RAF. He married in 1941 and flew out shortly afterwards to North Africa.

Douglas spent the first two years of the war fire-watching after work at Regent Street or Red Lion Square. He was also in the Gerrards Cross fire-service with his brother-in-law Ken Tremellen. Then at 39 he volunteered for the RAF, serving initially in Bomber Command at Uxbridge and Northholt.

But there was another and deeper reason why the war came as a blow to Austin. For the past seven years he had been a supporter of

Above: From the head down: a series of wartime advertisements.

91

Moral Re-Armament, the Christian revivalist movement which had swept through Britain in the 1930s.

Moral Re-Armament was the term used to describe the teachings of Frank Buchman, an American born in Pennsylvania in 1883. Buchman was that most rare and alarming of people, a man who endeavoured to live by the precepts of Jesus. His sincerity and goodness were overwhelmingly self-evident and his fundamentalist Christian message had an enormous influence throughout the world. He first came to England in 1927 at the invitation of a few Oxford scholars and by the early 1930s the Oxford Group had become very influential as a dynamic alternative to Communism, which had attracted many who despaired of the state of British society. Buchman did not decry Communism or any other political tendency. He just asked for total honesty, purity, unselfishness and love and said that God had a plan for the world to which every individual could make his or her own contribution. His message spread out like holy fire into every section of British society, including industry and government. Malcolm Muggeridge called it the only genuine religious revival of the period.

Austin was an early convert. He was deeply moved by the American's unaffected creed. He attended a number of Oxford Group meetings and began to reassess his whole approach to life. Buchman's appeal for self-knowledge created an irresistible urge for self-confession among many of his followers. Austin was no exception; at one meeting he found himself on his feet describing how he had overhauled the entire price structure in his shops because he was charging too much. It was a disclosure which revealed how profoundly he was examining his own principles. Always a relatively good employer, from then on Austin was determined to be a positively good one. An early result was the pension scheme, one of the first in the UK.

He wasn't slow to spread the Word to a wider audience. He invented a slogan of his own, 'Men before Money', and began to urge it on his friends and rivals in the menswear industry. His support for Moral Re-Armament was not without effect; he was, after all, a national figure, the model of the successful self-made man. A measure of his status was an invitation by the *Daily Mail* to join a panel consisting of Sir Harold Bellman, the ebullient chairman of the Abbey Road Building Society, Sir Edward Mountain, the powerful financier who headed Eagle Star Insurance, and Henry Williamson, the controversial author, to discuss the impact of the war on the middle classes. Austin only made a few contributions to the debate, but what he did say demonstrated a keen awareness of social disparities and an acute vision of the evolution of the British economy.

His first remark was a comment on the impression that evacuating the inner cities had made on the middle classes.

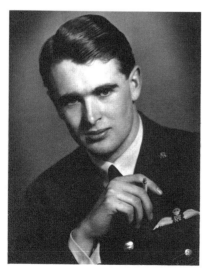

Kenneth John Austin Reed, Austin's younger son, was killed in action in October 1942.

A 1939 poster advertising service uniforms. Later in the war, making officers' uniforms became a large part of the company's business.

Take where I live, Gerrards Cross, though there are a thousand and one other places that would serve equally well. The average person in districts like these did not realize the dreadful condition in which thousands of his fellow-citizens were living, but the evacuation has opened people's eyes to a state of affairs which they are saying must quite definitely cease. A nation which can spend £6m a day on this war must be prepared to tackle these anomalies.

His final words embraced the future. Over 87 per cent of personal incomes in the UK were less than £250 a year, he said.

We must rethink the national position and evolve a system which will enable people who have not got purchasing power to acquire it, for not until they have shall we have real prosperity.

We have been living in an industrial age for only 150 years and we have done exceedingly well in that time. But I cannot help feeling that what we know as the British industrial age reached its zenith at the end of the last century. The signs of big social change are here. If we think we are going to finish this war and then put the clock back, we are mistaken.

In spite of his Christianity, though, Austin was unswerving in his patriotic support of Britain. Early in 1940 a neighbour dreamed up another slogan, 'It All Depends On Me', which Austin thought memorable enough to make a contribution to the victory drive, especially if reduced to the acronym IADOM. 'Its simplicity gives it power,' he wrote in numberless letters to his staff, the Government, the clergy

IADOM – 'It All Depends On Me' – was a slogan adopted by Austin to encourage his staff and others during the war. These are a couple of his ideas for posters.

ALWAYS CARRY SOMETHING WHITE
IN THE BLACK-OUT

and the press. 'It covers every phase of national activity, the services, the factory, the home front. Its scope ranges from simple saving of old paper and string to the most vital problems that have to be faced by the Ministers of State. It is the very opposite to passing the buck. Lived out nationally it will mean more planes built, more food grown, more savings certificates purchased, more guns made and the morale of the people stiffened for victory and freedom.' In spite of his enthusiasm, history does not record IADOM making a major contribution to the war effort.

Once again Austin was extremely supportive of members of his staff, both those serving in the Forces and the ones remaining in the shops. This time the risks were more evenly shared, due to the devastation caused by aerial bombardment. Many of Austin Reed's shops were damaged, several very badly, those in Coventry, Liverpool, Plymouth, and Southampton being totally demolished.

Summit House itself narrowly escaped serious harm in one of the early raids when St John's Church on the other side of Red Lion Square received a direct hit and was blasted to pieces. Douglas, who was fire-watching on the steps of the offices, was blown bodily backwards through the fortunately open doors and narrowly escaped serious injury. Part of Summit House was later requisitioned by the Government. Austin moved part of his reduced head office staff to the fourth floor of Regent Street and the remainder to temporary offices in Gerrards Cross, near enough to his home for him to cycle to work, at least in fine weather.

The crater left by the bomb which fell in Regent Street in September 1940 opposite the Austin Reed store. This photograph was taken the morning after the air raid; a crowd of people can just be seen kept back at the far end of the Quadrant. Roy Dyer, later retail display director, is one of the group of three, facing right, in the foreground.

MODERN MAN MODERN MAN

Spring 1940

The Regent Street shop, under the control of 'Bertie' Robertson, skirted destruction on a number of occasions. A delayed-action bomb in September 1940 blew all the windows out of both sides of the Quadrant, causing a vacuum which sucked all the shirts from the facing displays of both Austin Reed and Aquascutum. The first task of the returning staff of both shops was to sort out their respective stock from the pile in the middle of Regent Street. One piece of shrapnel bent the metal frame on an Austin Reed display-case without breaking the glass. There were no casualties, however, thanks to the volunteer watchman.

Austin himself had a near escape in July 1944 about which he wrote a few days later to Douglas, by then serving as a flying-officer in Iceland. A flying-bomb fell on the Regent Palace Hotel's annexe when Austin was walking across for lunch in the hotel's grill-room. He ducked under a shower of broken glass and returned to the shop to find only three windows broken. It was a fine day, the front doors were wide open, and the blast had dissipated itself in the well up to the third floor. The same afternoon another 'doodlebug' dropped near Australia House and smashed every piece of glass in the Kingsway branch. The staff and two RAF officers in the shop were warned by the roof-watcher and moved into the little stockroom in the back about

The lull in fighting in the first spring of the war is reflected in this peaceful cover of *Modern Man*. The magazine then ceased to be published for the duration of the war.

During the war, Austin Reed also produced women's uniforms. This advertisement is from 1942.

95

In the 1940s the replacement of bombed-out windows was restricted by law. The upper half of this window in Regent Street is being put to good promotional use.

five seconds before the explosion. Austin doubted that any of them would have lived if they had stayed.

But bomb damage was a minor problem compared to shortages of staff and, more seriously, stock. As before, Austin Reed recruited women who again proved more than capable, although once more there were occasions when relations between customer and shop assistant threatened to become warmer than usual.

More embarrassing for the male staff was the arrival of female customers. The first newly commissioned member of the Women's Auxiliary Air Force to call at the Leeds branch for her new uniform tested Austin Reed protocol to the limit, especially when she peeled down to her brassière in readiness for a fitting. Discreetly, Austin Reed's Mr Boydell handed the lady a complimentary shirt and decorum was restored.

Making officers' uniforms rapidly became a large part of Austin Reed's business, as supplies of civilian clothes dried up. It was another niche-market opportunity, as streams of young men emerged from

Perhaps the first display of women's clothes in an Austin Reed window, c. 1941.

officers' training camps with brand-new commissions and an immediate need for a complete new wardrobe. Other menswear shops were in the same situation, however, and competition for new customers was intense. Austin Reed met the challenge by opening local branches and by stationing salesmen near the camp to distribute leaflets detailing the company's range of full and service dress-uniforms, plus all prices from £25 for a khaki melton overcoat to 3s. for patrol collars (badges of rank extra). Over 40 varieties of women's uniforms were also made, each with its special style and requiring its own materials, buttons and badges.

Uniform production was initially based in a small cutting-room off the bespoke department in Regent Street, due to the fact that it was here the idea originated, but was soon transferred to Summit House. Conforming to the myriad particulars of the Armed Forces many uniforms proved a demanding test for the Austin Reed service and required a large number of visits to various headquarters to obtain the right details, with a mass of notes and trial patterns.

During the war Austin Reed made uniforms for admirals, generals, and air marshals. It also found itself engaged in some very 'hush-hush' work fitting out special agents and members of resistance groups with clothing of a suitable Continental cut for their dangerous missions. A number of Italian and German uniforms were also secretly manufactured by Austin Reed, with much of this clandestine work taken home by especially trusted members of staff to make sure even the cutting and tailoring of the fabrics went undetected.

The company's most famous customer was the Prime Minister, who asked if the Austin Reed service was up to producing a suit that could be put on in ten seconds, in the dark if necessary. The result was Winston Churchill's famous one-piece siren-suit. It was such a success that the great Englishman ordered a formal one in velvet, remarking that he didn't mind in the least if he was hailed as little Lord Fauntleroy. Austin Reed also provided Churchill with black silk 'blinker sashes' which he tied over his eyes to help his concentration when composing his wartime speeches and broadcasts.

As in the First World War, Austin Reed's business was badly affected in the early years, but rising prices contributed to surprisingly good figures in the later stages. The company was also buoyed up by the heroic efforts made by the staff, old and young, male and female, who along with the rest of the population endured shortages and privation with a determination that has become a legend.

But not without cost. When the staff returned to Summit House after the war, a bronze plaque commemorating Austin Reed men who had been killed on active service was dedicated and unveiled in their memory. The roll of honour contained nineteen names, including Kenneth John Austin Reed.

The Prime Minister's famous siren suits were tailored by Austin Reed, as were a number of his dress uniforms.

The memorial plaque at Regent Street commemorating all the members of staff killed in action.

Austin's younger son had been lost in combat over the Mediterranean in October 1942. It had been a terrible blow, one only made bearable by Austin's strong faith and the support of his family and friends, including Frank Buchman, who wrote immediately from Saratoga. The loss, combined with the burden of running the business, put a strain on Austin's heart. By the end of the war he was a sick man. He was in bed for the last three months of 1944 and had a longish spell in hospital in 1946. When he returned, it was perforce on a less continuous basis.

Business had to go on. It was a matter to which Austin had given a great deal of thought. His belief that the world was changing had if anything strengthened since his comments to the *Daily Mail*. As 1944 drew to a close, he wrote a letter to all his employees. 'People often ask me,' he said, 'what is going to happen to the business after the war? That question I cannot answer in detail . . . but this I do say even now with certainty. Conditions in business will never return to pre-war standards. They did not after the 1914–18 War and they will not after this one. There will be unaccustomed problems for every one of us to face, new developments to foster, new types of competition to counter and probably dramatically new types of merchandise to sell.'

The first problem that the end of hostilities brought, however, was not new merchandise but no merchandise. Demobilization produced a gigantic demand for civilian clothes which wartime rationing and controls made it impossible to meet. As Austin Reed's staff filtered back into the shops, they found themselves in the front line of what Austin called the battle of supply. They responded with the wiliness that only military life could teach. One of the most successful was Doug

The inside and front of the card sent to Austin for his 70th birthday on 6 September 1943. His sense of fun was well known and enjoyed throughout the company.

Davis, who had joined Austin Reed aged 18 in 1930 at 30*s*. a week and had been made manager of the Fenchurch Street shop on his return from the war. Davis's wartime experiences had included spells in Italian and German prisoner-of-war camps, from both of which he escaped, the first time to be recaptured in the Alps and the second, through Czechoslovakia disguised as a Lithuanian refugee, successfully.

Davis had already established himself as one of Austin Reed's most promising recruits before the war, inventing an effective method of stock-control for collars, which most branches still sold in vast quantities – it was nothing for a City branch to sell 300 dozen in a week, in a bewildering variety of shapes and quarter-inch sizes. He had also been one of the youngest members of the staff council and had become first its secretary and then its chairman.

Now in charge of his own branch, he quickly showed his talent for making the most of opportunities. In the early months after the war, stock was so desperately short that Austin Reed accepted anything it could lay its hands on, including suitcases and garden hammocks. The display department at Regent Street refused to put these aberrations in the windows, but Davis had no such scruples. Nor did he ask questions when an RAF pilot came in with a large roll of cream silk, brought in illicitly from Ireland. Instead he made him a dozen shirts and silk pyjamas for his forthcoming honeymoon with the actress Florence Desmond.

Davis also located a large consignment of white shirts in Austin Reed's temporary Plymouth shop designated for the Navy, which meant they were not available on clothing coupons. Helpfully, Davis accepted this unsaleable stock for his own branch, where of course

Dali-esque advertisement for Austin Reed, from *Modern Man*, 1946.

The northern branches held annual outings in the Peak District, which became known as the Cowslip Rallies. Tom Simmonds and Douglas can be seen in the middle at the back.

Jack Shorter modelling a dinner suit styled after Second World War battledress in the Modern Menswear Exhibition.

they remained unsaleable. But not, however, unswappable for coloured shirts that could be bought with clothing coupons. By the end of the year he had sold his small stock of coloured shirts many times over in exchange for white ones. He had also sold a surprising quantity of cuff-links, another stock item in reasonable supply, by the simple device of offering Saturday morning off to the salesman who sold the most pairs along with each shirt sale. Not surprisingly, Fenchurch Street topped the Austin Reed branch sales league for 1946.

The following year Austin Reed staged a modern menswear exhibition, which was opened on 2 June 1947 by Sir Stafford Cripps, President of the Board of Trade. From an idea of Hubert Taylor-Rose, the company's display manager, the exhibition grew to cover the whole of the first floor and included such dramatic devices as a sailing dinghy as a background for the beach wear and flowers and shrubs to give a summery atmosphere.

The clothes, too, were radical, with much use of dramatic patterns and racy colours, while such innovations as shirt collars with six-inch points and sports shirts worn outside trousers attracted great comment. There was a nylon foldaway golf suit in green, yellow, and rust, a leather jacket with tweed sleeves and a much-photographed dinner-suit with a battledress top modelled by Jack Shorter, Bob Shorter's son. The exhibition was televised and also shown on Pathé News in cinemas all over the country.

Sadly, this public relations coup did little to boost Austin Reed's sales, which were still limited by shortages of stock. It wasn't until 1949 that Herbert Kidson, who had taken over from Austin himself as chairman, could report that supplies were anything like adequate. Although profit margins were controlled by the Government, the rise in turnover meant that Austin Reed had made a record profit of

£242,000. A year later pre-tax profits had risen again, albeit narrowly, to enable the company to celebrate its golden jubilee in style. In the 50 years since Austin had started work in Reed & Sons's first City branch in Fenchurch Street, the company had acquired an un-rivalled reputation in the British retail menswear industry, with 30 branches across the United Kingdom, its own shirt factories in England and Ireland, a world-wide export business and total assets approaching £2m.

The 'A Peacock Sings in Regent Street' promotion in 1948 heralded the end of rationing and utility clothing.

101

9

'To Those of You Who Follow'

AUSTIN REED's celebration of its golden jubilee was muted by the fact that its founder was a sick man. Austin had, in fact, retired from the chairmanship in 1948 and he was no longer taking an active part in the company's affairs – at least, not officially. He remained intensely interested in every aspect of the business he had built up over so many years until his last days.

The 1950 summer issue of *The Tie* carried a special message from Austin in which he thanked all his employees for the contribution they had made. He picked out Herbert Kidson, who had succeeded him as chairman, and Bob Shorter, 'Willie' Williams the display studio manager, Percy Bone the hosiery buyer and Jack Martin who had run the three Liverpool shops throughout the war, all of whom had served for more than 40 years, for special mention, and regretted that he could not do the same for everyone who had worked for him for more than 25 years, as there were more than a hundred and twenty.

To those who were comparative newcomers, Austin said they were inheritors of a tradition.

> We who have built this business are not so much proud of its size – many businesses have grown to much larger dimensions in fewer years – as we are jealous of its reputation. The 'goodwill' of a business is its most valuable asset. It cannot be purchased with money. It can only be built into the fabric of the business by the application of sound principles and by patient service. Every transaction goes to the making or marring of goodwill. Every approach to a customer or a potential customer builds up or pulls down the reputation of the business. From the managing director down to the rawest recruit, we are all concerned with this vital force known as goodwill. It is the power that pulls us through difficult times. It has enabled us to withstand the shock of two world wars and successfully to weather the depression of the 1930s.
>
> To those of you who follow after us, I say let no word or deed of yours

Above: The new AR logo by Milner Gray was introduced in 1954.

Opposite: Poster painting by John Pimlott of the company's flagship store from the 1946 booklet 'For Men about Regent Street'.

detract from the reputation for fair and honest dealing, and willing and courteous service which our business possesses and which is your inheritance.

It was a restatement of the ethos to which Austin had adhered throughout his business career. His commitment to service before and above everything else was as undiluted as ever.

The message was also his valedictum. Four years later Austin Reed died, aged 80. From a national figure between the wars he had become a legend in his own lifetime. His passing, which was regretted throughout the national and trade press, seemed to mark the end of an epoch. Many people outside the company had been unaware that Austin Reed was still alive. Some post-war customers, indeed, did not realize that the name over the shops was that of a real individual. His death, however, seemed to threaten the very existence of the company.

In reality, Austin had not been part of the day-to-day management of the company for at least five years and, although the board was still led by his life-long associate Herbert Kidson, most of the senior posts had been taken over by a new generation led by Douglas Reed, who had become vice-chairman in 1947 and joint managing director in 1952 with Eric Collins. That year also saw the appointment to the board of Hubert Taylor-Rose, Derrick Kidson, Herbert's nephew and also an accountant, and Derek Chidell, Austin Reed's new company secretary. They were joined two years later by Tom Simmonds, another 1930 recruit who had inherited Percy Osborn's role as staff director.

Between them, the members of this group had been taking increasing responsibility for several years. Their promotion to the board reflected this. But a more significant reason was that some parts of Austin Reed had run into serious financial trouble and there had been something of a senior management shake-out. The cash crisis had been caused by overstocking. Immediately after the war shortages of supplies had

Austin and Emily at their home in Gerrards Cross.

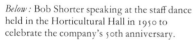

Below : Bob Shorter speaking at the staff dance held in the Horticultural Hall in 1950 to celebrate the company's 50th anniversary.

Austin Reed held an annual golf match with the partners of Pritchard Wood, the firm's advertising agency. The AR people in the picture are: back row, Claude Hills (third from left), Jack Evans (fourth from left), Bob Shorter and Dick Pierce (sixth and seventh from left); seated, Douglas Reed (left) and Lena and Herbert Kidson (centre); front row (centre) Ken Tremellen.

been Austin Reed's greatest preoccupation and every effort had been made to encourage increased production, particularly of shirts. To meet demand, the company had gone to great lengths to maximize its own purchases of material. The Korean War had had a dramatic impact on the cost of raw materials of many kinds, with wool prices tripling, and orders for trouser material had to be placed more than 15 months ahead. Cloth manufacture had recovered but with demand still outstripping supply the company had continued to press for as much shirt material as it could get.

Unfortunately consumer demand had fallen abruptly towards the end of 1951 and Austin Reed had found itself heavily overstocked. The situation extended to all its merchandise and Austin Reed had to dispose of excess stock by the time-honoured technique of cutting prices. The effect was a sharp fall in margins and a disappointed Kidson had to report a drop in profits from a record £244,000 to £142,000 for the year to 20 February 1952.

Austin and Emily, with Herbert and Lena Kidson, presiding at the company's golden jubilee dinner at the Dorchester Hotel in 1950.

A 1950s shirt advertisement shows the Omagh factory in Northern Ireland.

But worse was to follow. To its dismay Austin Reed discovered that it had failed to cut its supply contracts and had accumulated a huge stockpile of material, far beyond the capacity of the parent company to absorb. The only solution was to dump the excess and write off the loss, which amounted to something like £200,000.

The immediate blame fell on Dick Pierce, who had been made a main board director in 1939. Pierce controlled the buying of all shirt-ings for the Dalston Lane factory and the Omagh Shirt & Collar Co. in Omagh, Northern Ireland, in which Austin Reed had acquired a 49 per cent interest in 1948. It was a measure of the extent to which he was held responsible for the crisis that his resignation was only given a brief mention by Kidson in his chairman's statement in spite of Pierce's 38 years with the company. A year later Bob Shorter retired after 45 years with Austin Reed. They left behind them an organization which had very nearly been forced into receivership. Although Austin Reed's assets were far in excess of the losses, the company had found itself in a cash bind which the banks, tied by strict lending-limits, could not alleviate.

Not for the first time, Herbert Kidson came to Austin Reed's rescue. His Manchester-based firm of accountants had acted for Austin Reed from the very earliest days, from the time when Herbert was introduced to Austin by Frank Battersby. The partnership had other clients, how-ever, including Leonard Thompson, whose family owned the whole of Blackpool Pleasure Beach, then the biggest amusement-park in Europe. At Herbert Kidson's request, Thompson lent Austin Reed

106

£100,000 without security. (There was a footnote to the loan. After the formalities were agreed, Leonard Thompson decided to do a little shopping in the Regent Street store, only to have his personal cheque refused by the store manager on the grounds that he was not a known customer. Hastily the chairman authorized a deviation from the house rule.)

The crisis might have been averted, but it still highlighted the fact that much needed to be done within the group. Although Herbert Kidson deserved every credit for rescuing the company from its plight, he decided a year later that the time had come for his own retirement.

He was succeeded by Douglas Reed. Austin's elder son had been involved in the business for nearly 30 years and had been a director for 20. A quiet, unpretentious man, Douglas had inevitably been under the shadow of his famous and forceful father. But he had several invaluable attributes which made him, in the event, a remarkably effective chairman.

One was a fastidious sense of style which underwrote the continuance of Austin Reed's commitment to quality at a time when many of the pressures were to go down-market. Another was a willingness to delegate executive responsibility. A third was a talent for reconciliation, which defused management conflict. Douglas also had

This Ronald Searle cartoon, which appeared in *Modern Man*, emphasizes the importance of choosing the right tie. According to the accompanying story, the club secretary escorted the erring member to Austin Reed, where 'he chose a paisley pattern on a dark blue background'.

The opening of the new Manchester shop in 1956. From left: Hubert Taylor-Rose, Barry Reed (half-hidden), Douglas Reed, Eric Collins and Derrick Kidson.

All the shops mounted this special window display to mark the coronation of Queen Elizabeth II in 1953.

great personal charm and an untiring devotion to the well-being of every employee in the group. It was a deceptive combination that encouraged individuals throughout Austin Reed to maintain its traditions of service and quality, and generated immense loyalty towards the new chairman.

Among his supporters were Jack Evans, the lawyer husband of Austin's youngest daughter, Jane, and recently appointed a non-executive director, and a rising generation of Austin Reed managers, of whom Tom Simmonds, Jack Shorter, Claude Leaver, Bill Tindall, Derek Chidell, Hubert Taylor-Rose and Doug Davis were among the leaders.

Each was aware of shortcomings in his own area of the business. Davis was conscious that Austin Reed's antiquated stock controls and far from sharp-edged management systems needed overhauling. Simmonds, in charge of staffing, knew that manning-levels were too high and that there was a disproportionate number of rather elderly veterans. And Hubert Taylor-Rose, the company's new display director, was frankly dismissive of what he called the company's Edwardian attitudes to design, both in its shops and its merchandise.

To be fair to the previous management, the climate for private enterprise ever since the war had been far from easy. Kidson had complained constantly, along with the chairman of practically every other company in the country, of the rates of tax imposed by the Labour Government, especially the inequity of the punitive tax on dividends paid on ordinary shares, while profit margins had also been strictly controlled. But it was also true that many aspects of the business which had perforce been neglected during the war years had been been allowed to drift. Where action had been taken, it was frequently on the initiative of individual managers who had developed their own variation of the Austin Reed tradition. Many had done splendidly, but there was a clear need to reimpose a uniform system of management and a new sense of style.

Derek Chidell, who joined in 1950, had the dubious distinction of being a victim of the first post-war take-over bid, of a company called African City Property Trust, which had originally been formed to finance the development of Johannesburg. Newly redundant, he heard that Austin Reed needed a company secretary from his neighbour, Norman Westwood. As the board itself was already nervous about take-overs, he was an ideal choice. Both he and Derrick Kidson were to play important roles in Austin Reed's financial development in the future.

One of their first tasks was a hard look at the group's assets. The value of Austin Reed's property portfolio had become increasingly obvious for some time. Although Austin had never seen the collection of prime high street sites he had acquired as anything but a setting for his real business, selling men's clothes, the fact remained that many of them were extremely valuable. It was in recognition of this that a separate company, Austin Reed Properties, had been formed to manage the portfolio in 1948 and a more positive approach had begun to be taken.

In his first statement as chairman, Douglas reported that Austin Reed had bought the freehold of Summit House and of the large Bournemouth branch. He added that both had been professionally revalued at present market value. All Austin Reed's freeholds, he added, had been revalued since the war and the amount shown in the consolidated balance sheet represented their current worth.

The remark was a warning to potential predators. Following Austin's death there had been a flurry of speculation that the company might be the subject of a take-over bid. In fact, Isaac Wolfson and Charles Clore both made approaches. Douglas created various excuses not to meet or speak to them. It was a rumour that continued to crop up until Douglas finally scotched it, for the time being anyway, by revealing that over 50 per cent of the voting capital was firmly held by the Reed family, their close personal friends and employee share-holders. But the revaluation alone did nothing to rescue Austin Reed from its cash problems, which the loan from Blackpool had only defer-red. The answer to this was clearly to release some of the capital value of the property portfolio.

Fortuitously Austin had seized an opportunity during the war to extend his Regent Street leases even further towards Piccadilly. Called Victory House, this extension would, he hoped, eventually become Austin Reed's first women's store. But to date there had been no chance to pursue this grand plan.

The proceeds of the sale of Victory House helped resolve the financial problems arising from the shirt saga. At the same time, an even greater threat to the Reed family ownership of Austin Reed had been averted. Austin had neglected to take any precautions against death duties, which under the Labour Government had become punitive. And it was sadly clear that his chances of living for six years – the period needed to exempt his shareholdings from death duties by transfer of ownership – were very slim. Chidell came up with the solution, which was a single-premium life-insurance policy. The premium was painfully high, but the proceeds were tax-free. At Austin's death, two years later, the proceeds of the policy and a subsequent one were sufficient to meet almost all Austin's estate duty liabilities.

The new company secretary also claimed the credit for another tax-avoidance scheme which substantially cut its tax bill. The revaluation of the group's property had revealed just how much the value of its leaseholds, as well as its freeholds, had risen since they were first acquired. A particular example was Regent Street, where Austin Reed

A. E. Jury was the first employee after Austin to complete 50 years with the company. At this presentation he and his wife were given tickets for a cruise. From left to right: Bob Riddell, Barry Reed, Douglas Reed, Hubert Taylor-Rose, Mr Jury, Tom Simmonds, Derek Chidell, and Jack Evans.

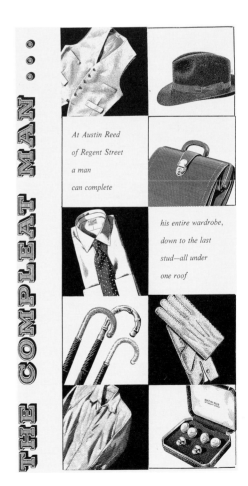

THE COMPLEAT MAN

At Austin Reed of Regent Street a man can complete his entire wardrobe, down to the last stud—all under one roof

An ambitious window display promoting
Tenova socks.

had a 75-year Crown lease on an almost nominal £13,000 a year rent
with 53 years to run. Chidell conferred with Derrick Kidson and his
firm's tax advisers. The answer was beautiful in its simplicity. Austin
Reed sublet its Regent Street premises to its pension fund for a rent
of £13,000 a year, incurring no tax liability and receiving a large tax-free
capital premium. All the pension fund's income, of course, was tax-free,
so nothing stopped it reletting the branch at a very much higher market
rent to none other than Austin Reed! Austin Reed, naturally, could
set this higher rent against income tax, and was also able to take its
tax-free capital profit on the deal into its profit and loss account over
the period of the lease.

The last manœuvre was to declare two classes of dividend, one out
of income and the other out of capital profits, and ask shareholders
to choose which they would like. The poorer opted for the former;
those paying higher rates of tax chose the latter.

Finally Austin Reed issued new non-voting bonus 'A' shares as a
means of distributing part of the capital gain to all classes of
shareholder.

It was perhaps the first large-scale sale and lease-back deal in the
UK and within a few years it was standard accounting practice for
almost every major company in the country in a position to take similar
advantage of the tax laws.

While the financial structure of the company was being revised, the
retailing business was also under review. Hubert Taylor-Rose was
particularly conscious that Austin Reed was lagging behind the times
in its merchandise and its branch design. A small, dapper man with
a natural talent for design, Rose had joined Austin Reed in 1930, when
he was instantly impressed by the standard of shopfitting. 'I went to
one of the older branches in the City which had been fitted out by
Percy Westwood and I remember how struck I was by its consistency.
Even the hooks in the fitting-rooms were by Westwood. The quality
was incredible.' However, if Rose never lost his admiration for Westwood's workmanship, he soon began to suspect Austin Reed's designs
were out of date, although the pre-war results showed that they still
satisfied the company's customer-profile, which leaned heavily and
profitably towards the upper-middle-class and the expatriate trade.

The new bespoke tailoring department in the
Prospect Room at Regent Street.

110

During the 1950s the Austin Reed style was
defined by the French tailor and artist, Delmar.
His drawings came to be as distinctive and
easily recognized as those of Tom Purvis.

Black and white houndstooth check packaging designed exclusively for Austin Reed by Milner Gray.

The redesigned corner entrance of the Regent Street store features Milner Gray's new logo.

Austin Reed had paid for Rose to study at the Central School of Art and Design in the 1930s, where he was smitten with terrific force by the influence of the Bauhaus. As his knowledge of modern design trends increased, Rose became more convinced that Austin Reed was out of touch. Several of the leading Bauhaus designers fled Hitler's Germany and were employed by Simpson, Piccadilly, one of Austin Reed's greatest West End rivals. Their impact was immediately obvious. Even Austin Reed's advertising, for so long the unchallenged leader, began to look old-fashioned to Rose.

After the war, in which he specialized in camouflage and aerial photography, Rose returned to Austin Reed to be put in charge of all design, including opening new shops, modernizing old ones, arranging in-store exhibitions and window-displays, as well as overseeing advertising. He also found himself Eric Collins's confidant, accompanying the joint managing director on his travels around the branches and overseas. Rose persuaded Collins that Austin Reed urgently needed to introduce a new sense of style. He was backed by Simmonds, as well as by Jack Shorter. A merchandising committee was formed under the chairmanship of Ken Tremellen. By the mid 1950s the effect was starting to show through, with a new approach to store design and merchandise.

It was about this time that a third generation of the Reed family began to exert an influence on the company. Douglas's eldest son, Barry, joined Austin Reed's head office after serving in Korea, where he was awarded a Military Cross, and gaining experience of the menswear industry at Harrods in the UK, in Europe and in North America. Apart from an innate drive and enthusiasm very reminiscent of his grandfather, Barry brought one invaluable attribute to the company's executive ranks – first-hand knowledge of what a young man really fancied in the way of dress.

Barry was soon made merchandise director in succession to Claude Hills, who had been flagging slightly under the responsibility after so many years with the company, and appointed to the main board in 1958. Eric Collins was still officially in charge of operations, although Douglas had become joint managing director, but there was already no question about who was going to take responsibility for the future of Austin Reed. Not that the company was doing badly under its present management. In his quiet way Douglas was presiding over renewed expansion, with new branches opening at an average of one a year (including Brighton, Exeter, Cheltenham, Leicester, and Cardiff) and a vigorous refitting programme throughout the existing network, in particular Liverpool, Manchester, and Regent Street, where the sale and lease-back had released over £250,000 which was promptly being reinvested in extensive modernization.

Austin Reed also reintroduced the subscription accounts which had proved so popular before the war and which allowed its customers to repay their purchases on a rolling twelve-monthly basis.

It was under Douglas, too, that Austin Reed acquired Harry Hall Ltd, a specialist in riding-gear, with a shop in Regent Street and a manufacturing subsidiary in Basingstoke. Under the management of the mercurial Sydney Barney, Harry Hall had built up its wholesale business to the point where it had 600 agents across the country. Douglas made a point of assuring these essential people that Austin Reed had no intention of competing with them by selling Harry Hall-branded merchandise in its own shops.

Austin Reed also increased its investment in Omagh Shirt & Collar, the company that had been making Summit shirts and pyjamas for the past ten years, to 75 per cent of the ordinary share capital, upping its holding to 100 per cent a year later in 1959. It was at this time that the shirt-making side of the business started to trade under the name of Stephens Brothers. Foreseeing the restriction on retail margins in wartime, Austin had acquired this wholesale company back in 1938.

Arthur Stephens, its founder, invented the first self-supporting socks. These had an elastic top with a cut-out at the calf for comfort and were marketed as Tenovas. In the 1930s the Tenova sock attracted the attention of the fashion-conscious Prince of Wales who granted Stephens his Royal Warrant as hosier. The company was subsequently to become hosier to King George VI, then to the Duke of Edinburgh and, more recently, to the present Prince of Wales. It also holds a Warrant as shirt-maker to Prince Philip. Armed with this valuable accolade and supported at the production end by Dick Pierce's son Austin, Gilbert Stephens, Arthur's son, found a useful market in America and elsewhere for Omagh's products.

But it was Barry that brought a new dynamism to Austin Reed. He quickly allied himself with the younger executives, especially Jack Shorter, with whom he developed a close working relationship. He questioned established attitudes and practices, often to the ill-concealed dismay of more experienced but too complacent people. And he looked with a fresh and wider perspective at the prospects for Austin Reed in the 1960s.

Harry Hall was the first manufacturer of riding wear to market and promote jodhpurs in stretch materials. These gave a better fit as well as greater comfort and flexibility.

BY APPOINTMENT TO
HRH THE DUKE OF EDINBURGH
SHIRT MAKER AND HOSIER

Stephens Brothers Ltd

113

10

A Cue for Change

T HE British have always been innovators when it comes to men's fashion, even as far back as the seventeenth century, when Charles II invented the original three-piece suit as a reaction to the flamboyance of French court dress. Of course, subsequent developments have changed it almost beyond recognition, but the roots are clear. Since then, the names of different garments establish the British origin of many modern menswear innovations, whether lordly from the nineteenth century – such as the Duke of Wellington's boot and the Duke of Norfolk's jacket, Lord Cardigan's cardigan and Lord Spencer's tailless coat – or more humble – for example, blazers, brogues, mackintoshes, jerseys, tattersall checks, the trilby (from a book by George du Maurier), Fair Isle sweaters, deerstalkers – the list goes on.

Many of these inventions have been popularized in other countries. The first major fashion change of the post-war years, the wide-shouldered drape jacket, originated in Britain but was developed by US tailors into the 'drape shape', with generously cut trousers. But there was a much more radical post-war evolution occurring in men's clothes – the demand for leisure wear.

It was James Laver, the clothes historian, who developed the theory that changes in fashion originate with sporting dress which in the process of time becomes everyday clothing, then formal wear, and finally servant dress. He cited the cutaway tail-coat to support his thesis, first invented for riding and ending up as the garb for head-waiters. The theory has its detractors, but it was one with which the tailoring industry felt perfectly at ease, as long as the changes were initiated from the top.

Much more difficult to assess was the demand for stylish leisure wear springing from the lower social strata. The whole idea that the working classes could be the arbiters of fashion was extremely hard to assimilate. Austin Reed found it as difficult as anyone. It was tempted to go down-

Above: The 1960s logo.

Opposite: The astonishingly strong influence of the 1960s resulted in the Cue departments. This is the original artwork by Alan Aldridge for one of the first Cue advertisements 'Introducing Cue Man'.

The classic Woodrow hat and Church's shoe.

This eye-catching display demonstrated Gannex's claim to be totally waterproof.

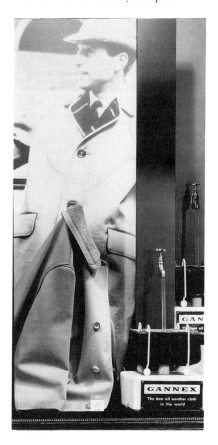

market, but not if it meant jeopardizing its traditional customers. But even they wanted to be in fashion.

Tentatively, Austin Reed began extending its range of merchandise with the inclusion of cellular cotton teeshirts, sharkskin swimming-shorts, zip-up wind-cheaters, and light-weight gaberdine sports trousers with Snugtex adjustable waistbands. It also introduced Church's shoes, Woodrow hats, and Gannex raincoats to cater for more conventional English weather conditions.

The choice of Church's shoes was inspired. Made from beautiful leather in traditional English styles, they were the nearest thing to handmade footwear that it was possible to buy and a perfect foil to Austin Reed's ready-to-wear clothes. The Church's concessions spread to every branch.

The Woodrow hats were less successful for the simple reason that headgear was going out of fashion extremely fast. It was a decline that the older men in Austin Reed found hard to accept. They all wore hats and longer-serving managers still insisted that their staff wore them, even if only in sight of the shop. And everyone knew that no gentleman went out without a hat. Apart from anything else, how could a man raise his hat to a lady if he wasn't wearing one? The demise of the hat was, in fact, one of the most definitive signs of a fundamental change in social attitudes in Britain after the war. In future, hats would only be worn in cold weather, or as fashion accessories. Austin Reed was not alone in persisting in the belief that hat sales must revive, but its Woodrow hat concessions never really earned their keep, while sales of bowlers, for so long a guaranteed stand-by, fell as inexorably as detached collars.

The Gannex raincoat was something else. It ranked with nylon shirts and socks as a garment of the future. Synthetics, it was obvious, would inevitably supersede natural fibres. It was only a question of time before scientists solved the technical problems and non-shrink, non-iron, everlasting clothing would oust wools and cottons for ever. It was surely only because synthetics were so new that old-fashioned products like wool and cotton still made better-fitting and more comfortable clothes. Not that everyone in Austin Reed was convinced about the superiority of man-made fibres, but to ignore them would have meant missing a marketing opportunity.

If all this sounds as though Austin Reed was out of touch with its customers during the 1950s, the growth of sales and the spread of branches proved otherwise. Until the 1960s, indeed, it could have been forgiven for believing that conditions were slowly but surely returning to normal, with the added benefit of a steady rise in real living-standards and disposable income. Throughout the 1950s the main problems facing the company were high rates of tax and rising wages – Austin Reed's employees, too, although as loyal as ever,

116

wanted to share in the general increase in affluence. One of Barry Reed's first battles was to raise salaries – particularly those of the buyers, several of whom were on the verge of leaving for more money.

Even the appearance of Teddy Boys, with their long, high-buttoned coats and narrow trousers harking back to Edwardian designs gave no warning of a radical shift in men's fashion. Nor did the abbreviated, close-fitting Italian suits which appeared in the early 1960s and were favoured by popular young musicians with strange names and pudding-basin haircuts. They might not be so flattering to the fuller figure, but they were still recognizably descended from those worn by their elders and betters. However, the habit of deference was clearly on the decline and young men were ceasing to look to their fathers for guidance on how to dress.

It is easy enough with the benefit of hindsight to recognize that the youth revolution of the 1960s was just the coming to maturity of the post-war generation, flush with the first fruits of the consumer society and convinced that none of the old rules applied to them. But at the time it was bewildering and inexplicable to many older people.

Barry Reed, however, was young enough to respond with enthusiasm and he hastened to push Austin Reed into this new market. It took a little time to work out a formula, but in September 1965 a new department was opened in the Regent Street store called Cue. Reporting this development, Douglas told Austin Reed's shareholders:

> I find it difficult to describe this to you in detail but its purpose is to cater for young men who like to dress in rather more advanced styles than normal. We have a special buyer for the merchandise, with a carefully selected selling staff and, to be frank, I have been quite surprised by the amount of business so far achieved in this small department. It means that we have got coming into our Regent Street shop men who we never saw before.

Nothing square about these suits

The inspiration for Cue was Carnaby Street, which had flowered into prominence at the beginning of the 1960s, revealing a huge pent-up youth market for male fashions which shocked the rest of the country both by its lively image and the teenage spending-power that fuelled it.

One of the first to ride the new wave was Michael Heseltine's magazine *Man about Town*, among whose early employees was a young man called Colin Woodhead. Woodhead came to Barry's attention by his outspoken criticism of traditional male clothing at the 1964 Harrogate menswear trade fair. Far from being affronted, Barry invited the iconoclast to lunch with himself and Jack Shorter, by now merchandise director, and offered him the job of setting up a department catering for the youth market.

Woodhead accepted and began putting together a new range. A complete amateur, he found it a hard task to convince Austin Reed's

Another early Cue advertisement. The photograph is by Helmut Newton.

traditional suppliers like Barran's of Leeds to lower waistbands, sew on belt-loops, taper trousers to the fashionable 14-inch bottoms, tighten arm-holes and sleeves, and generally incorporate all the subtle but essential refinements that would persuade the dedicated follower of fashion that he could even look at an Austin Reed suit. Woodhead was strongly supported by Hubert Taylor-Rose, who did much to help him convert his ideas into practice.

Creating the range of products was just the start. To succeed, the new Cue shops needed enthusiastic young salesmen able to put across the 'street cred' of the clothes they were marketing, and Woodhead soon found himself involved in training new recruits in the art of selling to the under-25 market. He was also closely involved in the advertising campaigns to promote Cue, which again by Austin Reed standards

The lively interior of the original Cue department in Regent Street.

were fairly outrageous in their intimations. A whole series of photographs, for example, were shot by Helmut Newton, already moving into his 'art' phase. The pictures broke new ground in men's fashion photography and did much to give Cue an image of its own.

The first Cue shop was immediately popular. What particularly surprised Douglas was the number of older men patronizing Cue. Austin Reed had been so encouraged by its success that they had put a Cue shop into the Knightsbridge branch and more or less converted the whole of the small Kingsway shop to younger styles, as well as putting in train plans to install Cue in at least nine provincial branches by the spring of 1968. In addition, Austin Reed had signed a contract with John Weitz, the well-known American fashion designer, to develop a wardrobe of travel clothes which, Douglas said drily, 'would be suitable for style-conscious men of all ages provided they had retained their figure'.

At the same time, a new expansion programme was embarked on to enlarge some of Austin Reed's provincial branches. The company also continued to expand its network, mostly by taking over established menswear stores, such as Hunter's of Blackpool, with branches in Blackburn and St Anne's on Sea, which was bought in 1967. This acquisition, incidentally, led to Austin Reed's first real taste of women's fashion, as it transferred Hunter's small St Anne's business to space in the local ladies' fashion store, J. R. Taylor, with Philip Taylor becoming a main board director of Austin Reed two years later.

Austin Reed also started to expand its export business on much grander lines, on the Continent as well as to the Commonwealth. The initial step was the formation of a new company called Austin Reed International to promote exports. Peter Reed, Douglas's youngest son, who, in the family tradition, trained abroad, in his case in Canada, Australia, and New Zealand, was given his first job in the group as manager.

Austin Reed's overseas business was given a valuable boost in 1967 when it signed a licence agreement with Hart Schaffner & Marx of Chicago, one of the biggest manufacturers of quality suits in the USA, to sell its clothing under an 'Austin Reed of Regent Street' label. For the first two years the new range was only sold through Hart Schaffner & Marx's own stores in the States, to gauge its acceptability, but then began to be offered to independent retailers as well. As well as providing Austin Reed with its first major 'brand' deal, the link with Hart Schaffner & Marx also provided a fruitful exchange of know-how between the two companies. As part of the agreement, Hart also acquired 14 per cent of Austin Reed's voting capital.

A by-product of increasing exports was the decision to build a modern factory at Lifford in Eire, where Austin Reed had taken over the Donegal Shirt Co. to supplement production at Omagh. The new factory, which benefited from liberal grants, opened in 1970.

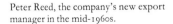

The man in the John Weitz Viyella shirt is John Weitz.

John Weitz used to promote his own range of leisure wear and travel clothes.

Peter Reed, the company's new export manager in the mid-1960s.

The group's new service centre at Thirsk in North Yorkshire.

A much more significant development, however, had been completed six months earlier. The need for a new headquarters had become more and more imperative and the board had decided to look for a greenfield alternative to Summit House. The search had finished at Thirsk in North Yorkshire. With Summit House in Red Lion Square worth £1 million and Austin Reed's Wembley warehouse also made surplus to requirements, the advantages of transferring most of the service activities out of London were self-evident. Thirsk was on the main British Rail line to Edinburgh and it was possible to drive all the way from the beginning of the M1 without a traffic-light, while the region was geographically in the centre of the UK.

Thirsk was also a delightful town, on the edge of a national park and with a pool of skilled labour. The only problem was persuading 25 or so key personnel in London to make the move. But Tom Simmonds took them and their families up for a long weekend and showed them the beauties of North Yorkshire, the spacious, handsome houses they would be able to afford – the local authority was even prepared to build new ones for them if they wanted – and introduced them to the local churches, hospitals, schools, and other amenities. Austin Reed also promised to pay all their expenses, not only to move to Thirsk, but back to London if they found they could not stand all that rural peace and beauty. Even so a few could not bring themselves to make the break, but of those who went, only one returned to London.

Douglas and Mary Reed after the unveiling of his portrait by James Halliday. Their second son, Laurance, is in the centre background.

The move was masterminded by Geoffrey Tubb, the company secretary, and took place in the autumn of 1969, including the new computer, which was craned bodily out from Summit House over the roof. Derek Chidell, as deputy managing director, also went to take charge of the transposed service centre, housing the accounts, warehousing, shopfitting, and training for the entire group. A new recruit as chief accountant was David Anderson, head-hunted for Austin Reed to modernize its management systems. The centre was opened officially by Mary Reed, Douglas's wife, on 16 April 1970.

The same year, Douglas was able to celebrate Austin Reed's fiftieth anniversary as a public company by reporting that turnover was over £8.6 million and profits had risen by more than 20 per cent to £600,000.

120

This in spite of mounting inflation and a series of economic crises in the UK which the year before had led the chairman to comment ironically that, as the country was apparently 'leaderless and penniless', it would be unwise to be too optimistic about the future.

The fact was, however, that Austin Reed's determined programme of branch redevelopment and expansion, the improvements to its manufacturing operations, the acquisition of Harry Hall, the export sales drive, and the success of Cue, had fuelled a resurgence which had more than consolidated the group's position.

More was to come. Barry and Jack Shorter were determined to extend Austin Reed's chain and in 1971 eight new shops were opened, including a large branch in Dublin, the first outside the United King-

The Reed family kept close links with the business. With Hubert Taylor-Rose are three of Austin's daughters at an in-store exhibition. From left to right: Phyllis Tremellen, Peggy Stephenson and Jane Evans.

Architect Norman Westwood (on the stairs) with Roy Dyer, the company's display manager, in the refitted branch at New Street, Birmingham. The same shop is shown on page 69 with its original 1930s interior designed by Percy Westwood, Norman's father.

The move to a more relaxed style of dressing prompted Austin Reed to suggest that the use of denim might be suitable for the office.

Wear your jeans to the office.

dom. In addition, turnover was given a boost by the decision to increase customers' credit from 12 to 24 times their monthly subscriptions. Harry Hall had been expanded by the purchase of Honorbilt, a trouser-manufacturer built up by Sidney and Jack Leader Cramer, and Austin Reed had also agreed to buy C. H. Ström, a Swedish retailer with shops in Stockholm and Gothenburg. The following year Austin Reed bought 80 per cent of Eduard Pelger, a Dutch retailer with branches in The Hague and Rotterdam.

A licence agreement had been signed with Bas y Cuguero of Barcelona and another a year later with Mitsui and Sanko Iryo to make Austin Reed jackets, trousers, and suits in Japan, while an Austin Reed department had been opened at Mitsukoshi, Tokyo's finest department store.

The Hart Schaffner & Marx licensing agreement had done so well that the Chicago company had formed a special division to market 'Austin Reed of Regent Street' and made Barry the president. One of the principal contributors to this success was Peter, who had spent two years in Chicago. On his return to the UK in 1971 he joined the group board as director in charge of the manufacturing division. Another new director was David Pearson, who was also a director of Austin Reed's merchant bank, Robert Fleming. Room was made for them by the successive retirements of Hubert Taylor-Rose, to be succeeded by Roy Dyer, and Tom Simmonds, both after more than 40 years' service.

Douglas, too, decided to retire from the chair in 1973 and accept the position of president. He had been chairman for 19 years, during which profits had increased nearly 15 times and turnover had passed £16 million. It had, he said, been a great privilege and real pleasure, but the time had come to hand over to a younger and more active man.

Jack Shorter (left), Eduard Pelger (centre) and Barry Reed, shaking hands on the deal to buy 80 per cent of the Dutch retailer's shops in Holland.

"Just say Skol"

I am an Austin Reed Woman, because –

*"Options has opened – a shop which suits my lifestyle.
My life is hectic.
I need a shop that specialises in my sort of clothes –
versatile and well made.
I've always liked the Austin Reed approach.
I expect personal service.
I can have my own account."*

I now find what I want from –

for today's woman at

AUSTIN REED

Floor 3, 103 Regent Street, London W1

11

New Options for Women

T HE younger and more active man was, of course, Barry Reed. As managing director he had been in effective charge of the family business for the best part of ten years and the results of his activity had been coming through for some time in the form of increasing profits and sales. In his first year as chairman he was happy to report record results for the sixth successive year, with sales exceeding £20 million and profits after tax topping £1 million for the first time in Austin Reed's history.

Barry was expanding the group as rapidly as possible. As ever Austin Reed was investing in its shops, but with a new policy of establishing outlets with a floor-space of at least 8,000 square feet in major provincial cities. The quest for new branches continued, but only in locations which could support a minimum sales area of 5,000 square feet.

The manufacturing side of the business was also doing well, with Harry Hall and Honorbilt integrated under the management of Sidney Leader Cramer and the two shirt factories in Ireland run by Austin Pierce.

Sales under the licensing agreements in the USA and Japan were expanding at an agreeable rate, while retail turnover in Europe was up by more than 50 per cent. Plans to open branches in Brussels and Copenhagen were well advanced, while Austin Reed's Scandinavian operations were being widened by the purchase of AB Cason-Kläder, a menswear business with stores in Malmö and Lund, founded by Carl Cason and run by his son Bengt, who was put in charge of all Austin Reed's Swedish shops. In 1974, too, a valuable freehold site was bought on Amsterdam's main shopping-street, the Kalverstraat, and a year later the whole of the Benelux operation was placed under the management of Eduard Pelger. One of his first moves was to open a Jaeger ladies' concession in the new Amsterdam branch. This experiment was so successful that within a year Austin Reed had repeated it in Stock-

Above : The current logo.

Opposite : The break into womenswear was accompanied by a clear statement of the company's target market.

125

holm and with Country Casuals in four UK branches. As far as the company could judge, none of its male customers minded in the least.

Nevertheless economic storm clouds were gathering. Although sales continued to rise, profits were hit by higher interest charges and positively massacred in 1975 by 20 per cent rises in pay and 33 per cent increases in rates. Emergency measures included increasing interest charges on subscription accounts to $1\frac{1}{2}$ per cent per month and selling off Swedish customer-accounts to a credit card company. Four smaller loss-making branches in the UK were also sold and Austin Reed disposed of some of its less-valued leases.

More worrying than the cash crisis was the drop in retail sales. 'Whenever family incomes suffer a decline, the first item to be affected is a man's expenditure on his own wardrobe,' Barry reported to the shareholders. But the company had hurried to limit the damage. It had made a close study of the steps taken by American retailers to combat a similar fall in turnover a couple of years earlier and identified several areas of potential growth. One was the continuing expansion in demand for leisure clothes and Austin Reed was placing greater emphasis on these in its Cue shops. Business on the Continent was difficult as well, while Stephens Brothers was having a bad time with its Irish manufacturing operations. Reluctantly, Austin Reed decided to close down the older Omagh factory in County Tyrone.

The result of all these measures was a strong recovery in profits. Honorbilt launched a new brand of men's slacks named 'Carter' and sales of 'Austin Reed of Regent Street' suits by Hart Schaffner & Marx positively boomed, with more than 140,000 sold throughout the US, while a new American licensee, Britannia Neckwear of Seattle, made a good start with an Austin Reed label.

Hart Schaffner & Marx created the highly successful 'Pub Crawlers' theme of advertising for selling 'Austin Reed of Regent Street' clothing in the United States.

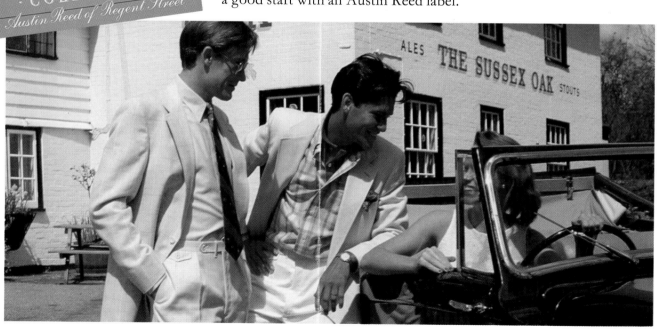

A Chester Barrie advertisement epitomizing the height of British quality and style.

Overall, Barry was reasonably confident. Although markets were difficult, there were signs that the tide of men's fashion was at last swinging back towards more formal wear. The wildest excesses of the late 1960s and early 1970s, the kaftans, the goat-skin coats, the flowered shirts, the sandals and bare feet and long hair, had vanished under the chill breath of inflation and economic uncertainty. Even the classless denim tide was beginning to recede. In *Summit*, the new life-style magazine for men launched by Austin Reed at the beginning of 1977, Barry credited the Englishman's innate sense of the correct dress for the occasion as being responsible for the triumph over Maoist uniformity. 'For good or ill,' he wrote, 'most of us have to work for our living and although we may enjoy our leisure, suits in our wardrobe are as essential as ever.'

The first cover of *Summit*.

That didn't mean that Austin Reed could afford to ignore fashion. The return to conventionality merely meant a new opportunity to

127

David Pearson, the group's deputy chairman since 1977.

'Mike' Reed, Barry's wife, with Myron Ackerman.

capture a share of the youth market, apparently more affluent than ever in spite of the traumas affecting the rest of the company.

The same year, 1977, Barry and the company suffered a heavy blow with the early death of Jack Shorter, who had done so much to re-establish Austin Reed's reputation for quality and style since the 1950s. Only a short time before he and David Pearson had been appointed joint deputy chairmen following the retirement of Jack Evans, as vice chairman, and Derrick Kidson. Peter took over as managing director of the retail division, having been personnel director for the previous three years. Roy Ward became his second in command.

In response to the new trends in fashion Peter Reed began hiring people like Elton John's favourite tailor, Tommy Nutter, to design clothes for Cue. It was evidence of the swing back to formality that Nutter produced an elegant range which combined fashion with restraint in the most admirable manner.

The highlight of 1978, however, was the purchase of Chester Barrie Clothes on 1 July. Chester Barrie was one of Britain's best-known suit-manufacturers, famous for the quality of its products. It had been founded in 1935 by Simon Ackerman, who had emigrated to the USA at the turn of the century, where he had built up a medium-price ready-to-wear tailoring business in and around New York. Chester Barrie was originally set up by Ackerman to make quality suits for the US market and the name was chosen because it sounded, to Americans at least, upper-class British. And Crewe was picked for a base because it had good rail communications with Huddersfield and the West of England, where the cloth was purchased, and Liverpool docks.

Ackerman's son Myron, fresh out of Yale with a degree in economics, was put in charge of the fledgling business, under the supervision of one of his father's most experienced colleagues, Arnold Shapiro. The war interrupted the company's progress but Chester Barrie survived by making uniforms, specializing in supplying American officers at the many US bases in the UK.

After the war the company switched back to making civilian suits to a high enough standard to win a contract from Harrods. Gradually Chester Barrie built up a reputation for very good quality ready-made suits with a high level of hand-finishing, made from the best cloth. Two brand names were used, 'Chester Barrie' itself and 'Simon Ackerman', which meant that the company was able to offer 'exclusivity' to competing retailers. Austin Reed was an early customer, with its first order placed by Douglas Reed in 1950, and the company soon became one of Chester Barrie's largest outlets. Chester Barrie expanded from its original workshop into spare capacity at Rolls-Royce's Crewe works, and then, when Rolls-Royce reclaimed the space, into a large factory of its own.

By the end of the 1970s Chester Barrie clothes were being sold throughout Europe by a team of agents who worked on commission, as well as in the United States, the West Indies – the company also had a cruisewear collection – and even as far away as Australia.

But in spite of his understanding of quality manufacture and his marketing flair, Myron, a large flamboyant man who chewed rather than smoked cigars and wore wide-brimmed hats, was too relaxed about financial controls and Chester Barrie was forced into receivership in 1978 due to unbridled expenses and a failure to limit production in line with the recession in retail sales.

Austin Reed was immediately interested. The 'Chester Barrie' and 'Simon Ackerman' labels were the best on the market and their loss would have been a tragedy. Other retailers were equally concerned and initially plans were floated for a consortium to rescue the stricken company. When these came to nothing Barry called a board meeting to discuss Austin Reed taking over Chester Barrie on its own. Sidney Leader Cramer was strongly in favour and did much to persuade the rest of the directors that the chance was too good to miss.

Terms were agreed and Austin Reed acquired the goodwill of Chester Barrie, along with its stock, its order-book, and its Crewe factory. All the employees had been served with redundancy notices by the receiver, but the new owners invited a selected percentage back immediately, among them Bert Barker, the production director, and Neil Fitton, the marketing director.

Fitton had been working for Chester Barrie for ten years, ever since his previous employer, a ready-to-wear tailoring company called Coops of Wigan, had been taken over by Dunn & Co. He had been very conscious of the real cause of Chester Barrie's downfall – uncontrolled costs – but had been a powerless spectator as a succession of efforts to control the company's spending had been blocked.

When a receiver from Coopers & Lybrand was finally appointed, Fitton was a close observer of his efforts to sell Chester Barrie as a going concern. And he was one of the people Barry Reed and David Anderson, by now Austin Reed's finance director, talked to about how much production needed to be cut back to make the company viable.

Less formal Chester Barrie clothes sell well in Europe.

Chester Barrie's substantial factory premises at Crewe.

Opposite: Options aims to dress the new breed of businesswoman.

Fitton estimated that he could sell perhaps 60 per cent, say 650 suits, jackets, and overcoats a week; pessimistically Anderson, a hard-headed Scottish accountant, nearly halved his figure to 350, a third of the pre-bankruptcy peak and Austin Reed's offer for the business was made on this basis.

Fitton already knew that he would be offered his old job, but it came as a complete surprise when Barry asked him if he would become Chester Barrie's new managing director. Fitton protested that he had never run a business before and that surely Chester Barrie's financial plight meant it had to be run by an accountant. 'You've got seven accountants already,' Barry said drily. 'That's not why you're in a mess.'

As soon as the purchase was completed, Austin Reed descended on Chester Barrie's Crewe works and gave it back its self-respect. Under the previous management it had been allowed to deteriorate into a shabbiness which offended every tenet of the Austin Reed tradition of quality; under its new owners everything was renewed or refurbished to the highest standards. Fitton was impressed; it was expensive, but the effect on the morale of the workforce alone made the cost worth while, not to mention the benefit to customer confidence.

In fact, with the company's debts removed and the workforce cut back in line with production levels, Chester Barrie went straight back into profit. With Fitton in charge, sales swept past Anderson's cautious minimum. By the end of its first full year as a member of the Austin Reed group Chester Barrie was manufacturing 800 sleeved units a week with production sold a full year ahead and exports accounting for 55 per cent of sales. The Duke of Kent, in his capacity as vice-chairman of the British Overseas Trade Board, made a special visit to the Crewe factory to congratulate the company on its success.

As a business, Chester Barrie had proved a brilliant acquisition. Its success was all the more marked as menswear manufacturing in general was having the greatest difficulty in making ends meet, under the pressure of high inflation and an overvalued pound. Apart from the advantage that Chester Barrie had gained from its restructuring, it was apparent that demand for its high-quality clothes was gratifyingly price-resistant. The top end of Austin Reed's own range of merchandise had shown the same resilience. Once again, the company's commitment to premium products was proving the right policy.

Another rediscovery was that demand for more conventional clothes stood up better than for less essential items when many people's disposable income was under pressure, as it surely was in the dark days of the late 1970s and early 1980s. London had become one of the most expensive cities in the world and there had been a severe slump in overseas visitors, with a consequent impact on sales, especially in Regent Street.

Austin Reed, however, had long learned that the answer to hard

Douglas celebrated his 75th birthday on 5 September 1978. A total of 750 people, including past and present members of staff, family and friends, attended a surprise party for him at the London Hilton. *Above:* Douglas cuts his birthday cake, a model of the Regent Street store. *Below:* David Anderson presents a hand-illuminated book inscribed with the names of those present.

Barry and Peter, photographed for *Vogue* by Patrick Lichfield, in front of James Gunn's portrait of their grandfather.

The Duke of Kent on his visit to the Chester Barrie factory in 1980. Sidney Leader Cramer (left) and Bert Barker (right) show him an example of the handwork in the garments.

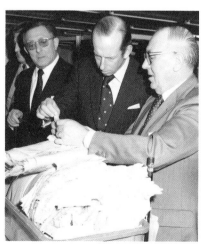

times was to try harder. It had redoubled its marketing effort and was investing, as always, in new display and presentation.

Quite why giving a branch a face-lift had such an impact on sales had always been a bit of a mystery. But time and time again Austin Reed had found that refurbishing a shop produced an immediate rise in sales. Perhaps it was that the activity generated a new dynamic throughout the entire operation, affecting not just the way that the branch looked, but the effort made to promote it through the media and the very demeanour of the staff. It was particularly true in Regent Street, where the store was in a virtually continuous cycle of refurbishment. And why not? If fashions in clothes changed every season, so too, surely, must the settings in which they were presented.

The latest development in Regent Street at the beginning of 1980 was Austin Reed's first venture on its own account into women's clothes. The experiment with Country Casuals had proved that a mixture of male and female fashion did nothing but good. But Austin Reed had never been entirely comfortable with the fact that another company was in effective control of part of its floor-space. Nor was it convinced that the Country Casuals range, good though it undoubtedly was, was quite compatible with Austin Reed.

Peter Reed decided to set up a separate Austin Reed women's department in 1979 and Gill Hewitt, a London buyer for Bloomingdales and other US stores, was recruited to run it. She was given a very clear brief; to adapt the American idea of dressing for success for British women.

What Austin Reed had discerned at an early stage was the emergence in the UK of a new class of career women who were beginning – not before time, many might say – to climb the executive ladder in the City and the professions. Like their male competitors, these women needed to look the keen, dedicated, serious part that senior managers demand of their aspiring subordinates, which meant eschewing frivolity and adopting a formal tailored style of dress.

Gill Hewitt had observed the trend at first hand in her own career. Appearances, she knew, counted a great deal when it came to obtaining jobs in industries like banking. But she also realized that many career-minded women were not really all that interested in clothes. What they wanted, whether they realized it or not, was the same pre-planned principle that underlay the male wardrobe. This did not mean copying men's clothing, but it did mean providing equally clear options. 'Options' – just the name for the new women's department of Austin Reed.

Hewitt divided her range into skirts, jackets, shirts, coats, raincoats, knitwear, trousers, dresses, evening wear, and accessories, and put 50 per cent of her budget into the first four categories. Ordering the first collection was exciting and demanding. She was trying to create something that was exclusive without being ephemeral. Where possible she went to existing Austin Reed suppliers, who by and large were fascinated at the opportunity to cater for women, but she also used her own connections in the women's clothing industry, as well as buying directly at fashion fairs.

THE WORKING WARDROBE.....

The first Options was given 3,800 square feet on the third floor of the Regent Street store and set a sales target of £10,000 a week. It seemed daunting, but to everyone's pleasure the new department easily surpassed its budget. Gill Hewitt introduced the very tailored body-shapes that were in vogue in New York, favouring grey and navy with velvet collars. They took off from the rails like fireworks. She was also one of the first to offer double-breasted jackets, something that had been out of fashion for men in Britain since the 1940s. Within three years one in three jackets sold in Options was double-breasted and by 1987 the figure was nearer 90 per cent. Hewitt was amused to see the trend reflected in Austin Reed's men's suit sales, although she reckoned they were two years behind her department in catering for the change in taste.

Since 1980 Options departments have been opened in every Austin Reed shop, with the latest in Aberdeen in 1988, by which time turnover for the division had risen to £11 million. Gill Hewitt confesses that, away from London, the range has had to be softened a little, with more emphasis on dresses and blouses. There have also been developments, like the trend towards the 'unmatched' suit, with contrasting jackets and skirts, as well as the development of niche-markets like 'Black at the Bar' for female barristers. Hewitt has maintained the distinctive formality of the Options collection, however, which has stayed strongly focused on the market at which it was originally aimed.

12

Response to a Changing Climate

LOOKING
THE PART

T HE beginning of the 1980s found most British companies in the same plight. A combination of circumstances, of which the main symptoms were poor productivity and runaway inflation, had pushed most of British industry to the brink of collapse. Many, especially in manufacturing, went under – in a period of something like four years 25 per cent of ICI's UK customers went out of business – and almost every company found itself faced with hard choices.

Predictably, many businessmen laid the blame elsewhere, particularly on the Labour Party, but that did nothing to resolve their problems. The only solution, it transpired, was to haul themselves up by their own bootstraps – and quickly. It was a time for heroic measures, which for many large companies meant abandoning their cosy managerial habits – in truth, as much responsible for their difficulties as anything else – and taking a much tougher approach to the business of making money.

Austin Reed was no exception, although it was, in comparison with many companies, in good shape. Its finances were very sound, labour relations were good, and productivity was relatively high. The lessons learned over three generations building up one of Britain's best-known and most highly regarded high street retailers had imbued Austin Reed with an indelible awareness of the importance of such basic business virtues as customer care, a positive cash flow, and the overriding importance of adequate margins.

This did not, however, stop it running into difficulties. No company is an island and Austin Reed found itself under pressure at both ends, with suppliers either failing or putting up their prices and many customers, themselves in financial straits, economizing on their wardrobes. The crunch came in 1980, the eightieth anniversary of the founding of the business. Barry Reed reported that weak customer-demand had affected Austin Reed throughout the year, with Regent

Above: The 'Looking the Part' campaign was a staff training programme introduced in the 1980s to re-emphasize the company's commitment to customer service.

Opposite: The tangibility of the textures in this advertisement perfectly reflects the renewed commitment to quality.

135

Colin Evans (left) and Neil Fitton stepping out in the company's logo.

Street and Knightsbridge the worst affected due to the absence of foreign visitors, scared off by the strength of sterling.

However, 'it is in a recession that we often learn most about how to make improvements in our business and to come out of it more strongly as a result,' the chairman said bravely.

The good news in the year was the continuing success of Chester Barrie, which was proving to be an inspired addition to the group. Much of the credit was due to Neil Fitton, who had rapidly demonstrated that he was an excellent manager as well as a natural salesman. Fitton had already expanded Chester Barrie's sales in the USA and Europe and the new subsidiary's contribution to group profits was proving something of a life-saver as the retail division struggled. He also renewed his contacts in the Far East and Australasia. While in Sydney, incidentally, Fitton called on another of Austin's grandsons, Colin Evans. Colin had previously worked for Austin Reed and, with Barry's approval, Fitton offered him the job of sales director for Chester Barrie. Evans accepted and returned to England to find that when Fitton said work, he meant it. The business day at Chester Barrie's Crewe factory began at 7.30 and when Colin arrived half an hour late on his first day Fitton told him that if he was ever late again, he would be fired on the spot.

Uncomfortable as Fitton's zeal might be, it was clearly the right medicine and in July 1980 Barry invited him on to the main board.

Overseas licence income had also risen and Options was proving a success, with the credit shared between Gill Hewitt for managing the ladies' department so well and Peter Reed for supporting it. It was partly because his judgement had been vindicated with Options that Peter was able to persuade the board to back another idea of his, the separation of Cue into a chain of free-standing shops.

Cue had become a significant part of the group, with 31 Cue shops in existing branches and the new season's collection of Cue 'Younger by Design' clothes selling well. Breaking Cue out into a distinct busi-

136

ness on its own was clearly a gamble, but it seemed a reasonable one.

In spite of the recession, Barry Reed was still in an expansionist frame of mind, with his determination only sharpened by the closure of two unsuccessful branches. In July 1980 he bought a country clothing business called Bladen, to augment the Harry Hall range and boost production at the Basingstoke factory, and early in 1980 Austin Reed also acquired the leading menswear retailer in Northampton, Swann's of Gold Street, and a chain of nine shops in Scotland which traded under the name of Edwards Sir.

The first half of the following year saw a desperate struggle to make profits and Austin Reed, like many other companies, undertook a major review of itself, subjecting each part of the group to a stringent appraisal of its profit potential. The immediate outcome was the closure of three more branches, staff reductions in both retailing and manufacturing, and the sale of Austin Reed's three Swedish stores. It was the beginning of a process of rationalization that continued with the closure of the Dublin store, which had been made unprofitable by huge rises in rent and rates, and of Honorbilt's small Nuneaton trouser-factory.

But not all was retrenchment. Stephens Brothers, for example, had acquired a second factory, at Bispham, near Blackpool, to meet demand for its ladies' shirts, and Austin Reed had also decided to open a new 20,000-square foot factory next to Chester Barrie to make what were described as 'quality-engineered clothes' using modern manufacturing technology. The new factory began by making garments for Harry Hall, Bladen and Phillips & Piper, another well-known country label bought by Austin Reed the year before.

The success of the new factory and increased demand for quality clothes bearing a 'Made in England' label, however, persuaded the group that it was missing a wider opportunity. The first 'Austin Reed of Regent Street' collection of ready-to-wear suits, overcoats, jackets, and trousers was test-marketed at the end of 1983, and by the end of 1984 the new clothes were being sold by Burberry, Gieves & Hawkes, Harrods and Scotch House, as well as in the group's own stores.

Barry was also able to report that Austin Reed had clawed its way back to the 1980 profit level. A year later he happily unveiled a new record trading-profit of nearly £4 million. Regent Street and the other London stores were making good profits again and all the main-stream businesses of the group were doing well, including the three independent Cue shops. The country-wear division was not having such an easy time, however, the three Dutch stores had been struggling, and the Scottish venture, Edwards Sir, had failed to live up to expectations and had been sold.

A year later and the group had introduced Options into 34 Austin Reed shops and opened nine free-standing Cue shops. New offices and

Sanko Iryo's stylish publicity for Austin Reed in Japan. The Japanese slogan (*below*) reads 'Orthodox Dandyism'.

正統派ダンディズム。

warehousing had been added to the Crewe factory, which could now handle the Harry Hall business as well as the new 'Austin Reed of Regent Street' range, a fourth Dutch branch had been opened at Arnhem and a small Chester Barrie shop was planned for Savile Row, a sign of the continuing success of the Crewe subsidiary.

But the cost of these developments had made Austin Reed look even harder at returns on its various activities, with six Austin Reed branches closed because they were dragging down the overall performance of the retail division.

Nevertheless demographics and style trends were, Barry thought, moving in favour of Austin Reed. 'The baby boom of the late 1950s is now leading to a growing population of over 25-year-olds, most of whom wish to dress in a smart but dignified manner in keeping with their profession or work,' he revealed. Sales of suits and other tailored clothing were rising, plus those of formal shirts and other accessories, both for men and women.

Although Austin Reed remained convinced that quality leisure-wear was a logical extension to its product range, it was beginning to become obvious that the Thatcher revolution in attitudes to work was causing

Showcard for the Stephens Brothers luxury range of shirts for men and women.

The continent of Europe is the main market for Austin Reed International. One of those involved in promoting a young, sophisticated look has been Joanna Reed-Ödner, Barry's daughter.

138

a return to more formal habits of dress. It had taken more than 20 years, but the pendulum had finally swung firmly back to the traditions of dress which the group had always believed in at heart.

To a certain extent, Austin Reed had always found it hard to accommodate informal fashion trends. Its whole success had been built on clothing the professional man and, while it had managed to survive and even prosper in the more egalitarian 1960s and 1970s, it had somehow never felt in total control. Indeed, there had been moments when it feared that egalitarianism was going to undermine formal business dress entirely, at least as a viable market.

However, far from passing away, the old order was suddenly back with a vengeance and men and women were dressing accordingly. It was almost like returning to the first days of Austin Reed, when every ambitious youngster aped his betters and the arbiters of everyday dress were men of propriety and property.

There were, of course, differences. Modern technology had transformed the way clothes were made. Synthetic materials held their shape much better and wore much longer. Air-conditioning and central-heating had resulted in suits becoming much lighter. Compared to the beginning of the twentieth century, in fact, men's and women's clothes were much more efficiently and precisely made and looked much smarter. But their function as indicators of conformity and aspiration was once again identical.

The sea change in social attitudes had, inevitably, a powerful impact on Austin Reed. To begin with it was reflected, as the chairman had already reported, in improved sales for suits and other formal dress. When it began to become obvious that the change was more than a fashion quirk, but was a symptom of a fundamental change in attitudes, it did much to clarify Austin Reed's business strategy.

Although it was obvious that it would always make sense to have a broadly based group, the greatest opportunities for profit and growth lay once again in catering for the professional market – which, as the expansion of Austin Reed's exports and licence income had shown, had become international.

Acceptance of this strategy put the whole of Austin Reed's operations in a new and simpler light. Both the Harry Hall and Honorbilt businesses, for example, were obviously peripheral to Austin Reed's main market and were disposed of. The group's product range, however, lacked high-quality knitwear and J. A. Robertson & Sons of Dumfries, the old-established manufacturer of cashmere and other top-quality sweaters, was bought at the beginning of 1986.

The free-standing Cue shops were also closed. Although the Cue departments for younger men's fashions continued to do well within Austin Reed branches, the reaction to more formal business wear had undermined the profitability of this sector of the market. Chester

Robertson of Dumfries, the group's knitwear company, was one of the first winners of the British Apparel Export Award, instituted in 1986.

Robertson's knitwear is largely sold under the Drumohr label. Over 90 per cent of the sweaters are exported.

139

1989

Two of the group's companies have won the Queen's Award for Export Achievement: Robertson of Dumfries in 1987, and Austin Reed International in 1989.

Colin Wilson, managing director of Austin Reed International, receives the British Apparel Export Award from the Princess Royal, president of the British Knitting and Clothing Export Council. Barry looks on in his capacity as chairman of the Council.

Barrie, on the other hand, was doing almost indecently well under the management of Colin Evans, who had been made managing director of the booming subsidiary and elected to the group board in July 1986.

At the same time Neil Fitton took over as group managing director from Barry, who became executive chairman. It was an appointment which recognized the extent of Fitton's contribution to the expansion of Austin Reed internationally. This move was a personal disappointment to Peter Reed and, sadly, he left the company a year later. He and his family now live in New Zealand, his wife Fran's homeland, where he has an interest in a menswear business.

The way in which Austin Reed responded to the crueller but more stimulating climate of the 1980s has been reflected, in the final analysis, in the figures. From 1982 onwards the growth in sales and profits was quite startling, more than 25 per cent compound on average, with new records established every year to reach a record of £80 million in sales and £8 million in profits in 1989.

In the same period Austin Reed's business has been precisely defined as a specialist manufacturer and retailer of top-quality clothing and accessories for men and women. The flagship of Austin Reed's retail operations is still the Regent Street store, supported by more than 40 branches throughout the UK, plus 11 Cashmeres of Scotland shops in the USA.

Austin Reed's principal brand names, Austin Reed of Regent Street, Chester Barrie, Drumohr, and Stephens Brothers, have become a major part of its business, with the clothes carrying their labels made in modern factories in England, Scotland, and Ireland. By any standards, Austin Reed is a significant international operation making a substantial contribution to the economy and reputation of the UK. It has come a long way from its beginnings in a single small shop in the City of London 90 years ago.

But it has not abandoned the principles on which it was founded. The new professionalism which has been a feature of the last ten years has extended throughout the two thousand or so people who make up the real assets of the group, but has done nothing to dilute the commitment to quality products and customer care that has underwritten Austin Reed throughout its history.

General Subject Index

(Figures in italics refer to illustrations)

Index of People

(*Figures in italics refer to illustrations*)